Making Out-of-School-Time Matter

Evidence for an Action Agenda

Susan Bodilly, Megan K. Beckett

Prepared for The Wallace Foundation

RAND EDUCATION and RAND LABOR AND POPULATION

The research described in this report was conducted by RAND Education and RAND Labor and Population for The Wallace Foundation.

Library of Congress Cataloging-in-Publication Data is available for this publication.

ISBN: 0-8330-3734-X

The RAND Corporation is a nonprofit research organization providing objective analysis and effective solutions that address the challenges facing the public and private sectors around the world. RAND's publications do not necessarily reflect the opinions of its research clients and sponsors.

RAND® is a registered trademark.

Published 2005 by the RAND Corporation
1776 Main Street, P.O. Box 2138, Santa Monica, CA 90407-2138
1200 South Hayes Street, Arlington, VA 22202-5050
201 North Craig Street, Suite 202, Pittsburgh, PA 15213-1516
RAND URL: http://www.rand.org/
To order RAND documents or to obtain additional information, contact
Distribution Services: Telephone: (310) 451-7002;
Fax: (310) 451-6915; Email: order@rand.org

Preface

The need and desire for a supervised setting and activities for children and youth during nonschool hours that contribute positively to their progress toward productive adulthood has grown over the last several decades. Interest groups, including school-age child-care providers, youth-development experts, educators, criminal- and juvenile-justice experts, and poverty experts, have called for increasing public support for or improving the quality of out-of-school-time (OST) programs. Some improvement suggestions are modest (requests for expansion of child-care programming to more needy families); others are more ambitious (that programs can and should aspire to improve academics, reduce crime, prevent unsafe behaviors, and/or improve social interactions). Stakeholders in this conversation offer varying pieces of evidence to support their cases.

Seeking to engage the public in an informed dialogue over the needs for and the effectiveness of improving or spreading OST programming, the Wallace Foundation asked the RAND Corporation to conduct a broad-ranging literature review to identify, frame, and assess the relevant issues in the OST field.

This report presents the findings of that review. We identified and addressed several major issues: the level of demand for OST services, the effectiveness of offerings, what constitutes quality in OST programs, how to encourage participation, and how to build further community capacity.

The audience for the report is policymakers, providers, and users of services interested in improved formal programs for OST and possible ways to expand provision.

The research was undertaken by staff in RAND Education and RAND Labor and Population as part of their mission to provide objective policy analysis and effective solutions to address the challenges facing public and private sectors.

The research sponsor, The Wallace Foundation, seeks to support and share effective ideas and practices that expand learning and enrichment opportunities for all people. Its three current objectives are to: strengthen education leadership to improve student achievement; improve out-of-school learning opportunities; and expand participation in arts and culture. For more information and research on these and other related topics, please visit its Knowledge Center at www.wallacefoundation.org.

Contents

Figures and Tables

Figures

Tables

Summary

Programs that offer out-of-school (OST) and out-of-home services to children and youth can be found in every state and locale and run the gamut from school-age care services supporting working parents, to programs specifically structured to prevent problematic behaviors such as drug use or teen pregnancy, to academically oriented programs designed to improve test scores, to those directed at supporting specific hobbies and interests.

A loosely connected set of providers, clients, sponsors, and intermediaries make up the local markets referred to as the OST field. This field and the actors in it have been evolving in response to shifts in the economy, the growing demand for services associated with increased numbers of working mothers in the labor force, concerns over youth development or the lack thereof, and increased academic expectations for youth.

While public interest in OST programs has waxed and waned in the United States for more than a century, the past 20 years have been unprecedented in the growth of provision and the amount of public financing for these programs. In the past 20 years, interest groups such as school-age child-care practitioners, youth-development experts, educators, criminal and juvenile justice experts, and poverty experts have argued that OST programs are part of a solution to problems they see besetting children and youth. These groups have successfully drawn attention to OST issues and worked to increase public funding, but they do not all agree on how to move forward.

Some voices in recent debates over the future of the field say it is enough for the marketplace to offer school-age care services during times when parents or relations are not available to supervise children. Others call for making subsidized programming more widely available. Still others insist on more ambitious programming to meet a range of goals, such as improved test scores or reduced crime. Some want OST providers to be entrusted more than ever before with the academic skill building of our children, holding specific programs responsible for improving test scores. Others favor these programs as havens from the academic pressures of schools, where children can learn social skills and develop mentors and role models to help them in their difficult circumstances. Finally, the role of government has grown to support service provision, and with it has come increasing regulation, accountability, oversight, and concern over meeting more ambitious goals, including improved academic test scores or reduced crime rates.

The Research Purpose

The Wallace Foundation, an active supporter of programs in this field, asked RAND to provide an objective and systematic examination of the OST literature to clarify and inform the key issues in the ongoing debates related to whether and how to improve OST programming. RAND undertook a broad literature review to capture what is known with some certainty and what is more speculative about claims being made. This report, the outcome of that review, investigates five major issues:

- the level of unmet demand
- the state of knowledge about the types of outcomes that participation in OST programs are expected to impact and the nature of the impacts observed
- determinants of quality in program offerings
- determinants of participation and selection
- practices effective in ensuring that quality programming is available to meet local demand.

The audience for this report is those active in improving OST services. This includes service providers, intermediaries, philanthropists, and policymakers. It can be used as a reference for them on the above issues, the current state of knowledge about those issues, and the strength of the evidence base for that knowledge.

We use *youth* to refer to the period extending from entry into school through adolescence (approximately ages 6–18). We define the subject of this examination as the available literature on public, group-based programs for school-age children that minimally provide care during non-school hours, but might also attempt to improve their behavioral, social, and academic development outcomes. Many of these types of programs are offered by community organizations outside the home, such as Boys and Girls Clubs, YMCAs and YWCAs, parks and recreation departments, after-school programs, libraries, and museums.

Findings from the Literature

The review generated the following findings.

Demand for OST Services

A significant debate over the provision of services concerns whether or not there is pent-up demand for programming. Some advocates claim significant pent-up demand for OST provision and call on policymakers to pass legislation providing public funding to ensure universal coverage. The current trend is to push for capacity expansion, seeking to offer more slots to meet unmet demand.

More children than ever before are in formal program settings before and after school, oftentimes providing only child-care services. Our review, however, found that the limited number of studies documenting unmet demand for services (1) were based on unfounded assumptions that cannot be verified; (2) often estimated the total possible needs for child-care services, rather than what was demanded from providers outside the home; and (3) were based on surveys that do not force the respondent to consider trade-offs in the use of funds, thereby probably overestimating true demand.

In contrast, studies of existing programs indicate significant numbers of open slots and dropouts, implying unmet demand for existing programs is not insistent or pent-up. We did not find systematic evidence of what it is parents and youth are demanding: a safe environment, improved or better social behaviors, improved academic outcomes, or all of these. We conclude that demand for OST programs, other than very general current-usage statistics, remains very unclear.

Potential Effects of Programs

We examined evaluations of OST programs to determine what outcomes they have been able to accomplish. Compared to the total number of programs operating, very few have been evaluated. The safety of children in OST provision has not been the focus of many program evaluations; rather, evaluations have focused on effects on academic achievement, academic attainment, and social behaviors. Children who choose to attend OST programs might differ systematically from those who choose not to attend in terms of motivation, aspiration, and other factors. A strong research design would control for this self-selection bias into the program to isolate its effects from the effect of the program. Most of the studies reviewed did not control for self-selection bias, making it difficult to conclude that differences between participants and nonparticipants are wholly attributable to program effects.

Analysis of the research with the most rigorous designs suggests that the few programs that have been evaluated have, at best, had modest positive impacts on academic achievement, academic attainment, and social behaviors such as reduced drug use or pregnancy. Documented academic and behavioral program effects sometimes varied by grade level, background of children, level of participation, program content by site, and whether the program developed was well targeted toward the desired outcome. These evaluations provide few insights into whether existing programs on average offer a safe and healthy playtime environment that might satisfy the demands of parents. There is no way of knowing if the average program offered would have similar academic or behavioral effects to those in the programs studied. The cost-effectiveness of these programs, compared to other interventions, including expansion of the school day, is not well understood.

Program Factors Associated with Positive Outcomes

Studies of what features of programs are associated with better outcomes are often not rigorous and depend on expert opinion. We drew on recent compendiums or studies of quality indicators in OST or related settings such as school-age-care literature, youth-development literature, effective-school literature, analyses of class-size-reduction programs, and recent studies on teacher-training effects.

There appears to be a convergence of these multiple, but less rigorous, sources on several program factors that might be associated with improved youth outcomes:

- a clear mission
- high expectations and positive social norms
- a safe and healthy environment
- a supportive emotional climate
- a small total enrollment
- stable, trained personnel
- appropriate content and pedagogy relative to the children's needs and the program's mission, with opportunities to engage
- integrated family and community partners
- frequent assessment.

We note that the field itself has moved toward the development of standards for service providers with the publication of standards consistent with the above characteristics. These factors have not been formally tested in OST programs or tested for effectiveness in rigorous experimental studies, but provide a useful cluster of characteristics upon which to base initial program-improvement efforts. These improvement efforts should be evaluated to determine whether in fact they are effective in meeting program outcomes.

Improving Participation

If quality programming is provided, then it might be appropriate to consider how to improve participation and, especially, how to target those children and youth who could most benefit from the services. We drew on a cross-section of fields to understand how to encourage and target participation. In recent years, leading behavior theorists have reached a consensus regarding the most important factors that determine how people choose to behave, which in turn are influenced by a host of individual, family, social, and environment factors. Other fields have made excellent use of these behavioral theories to target or increase participation.

We found empirical evidence that participation varies by participant background, implying that targeting services might increase participation. For example, lower-income families might be more attracted to subsidized programs that are located within their neighborhood and convenient to attend.

Practical ways to increase enrollment and attendance in programs have been developed and tested in the job-training and military-recruiting fields. Proven or promising ways to bolster enrollment rates in these fields include identifying all possible participants, dedicating sufficient and effective resources for outreach and recruitment, locating such efforts in places where targeted youth and their key influencers congregate, and combining advertising resources across like organizations. Monitoring attendance and quality, following up on absentees, and offering incentives to programs for achieving high attendance rates are potential ways to improve attendance. Most importantly, to successfully target a group and provide accessible services requires knowledge of their needs at the local level.

Improving Community-Level Provision

While often written about, we found little rigorous empirical evidence about how to build capacity in the OST field. Studies did provide notions about how to improve and build capacity both of individual programs and across local, regional, and national markets. In general, the review pointed to a few approaches that can be debated, but did not provide the evidence needed to create a well-crafted agenda.

- Strong arguments were uncovered that point to the effectiveness of more-integrated approaches with collaboration, joint planning, and networking as important ways to further the debate, as well as

identifying shared challenges, best practices, and common interest among the groups involved.

- Historic examples reviewed showed the importance of data collection and analysis, data-driven decision making, evaluation, self-
assessment, standards, and quality assurance to the development
of other relevant fields.
- More-generic discussions pointed to the need for better incentives
for improved performance, accountability mechanisms, and perhaps market-based relationships to engage competition as a way
to increase performance.

Implications

Policymakers and program implementers should remain skeptical of
claims about pent-up demand for programs as well as claims that these
programs can meet multiple needs and impact positively on multiple
outcomes. Rapid growth should make way for concentrating on how
to improve the quality of offerings by existing programs and of systems
of provision.

A public discussion of the goals of OST would benefit from a
better accounting of real demand, both in qualitative terms (what do
children, youth, and parents want in OST programming?) and quan-
titatively (how many slots are demanded for different goals?). The first
steps in that direction are survey-based local-area assessments of demand, and then matching program content and support to those specific needs. Resources would be well spent in assessing local needs and
barriers to participation and developing programs to meet those needs
and remove those barriers. Furthermore, any push toward rapid expansion of slots should be tempered with an assessment of how that expansion in quantity might affect the quality of the programs offered. The
opposite might also be true: improvement in program quality could
have the effect of increasing demand.

Policymakers should be cautious about overly optimistic predic-
tions of the effectiveness of OST programming for improving youth
outcomes such as test scores and improved social behaviors. Much de-

pends on the specific characteristics of the program and youth who participate. While programs have been developed that have modest positive effects on academics and social behaviors, there is no evidence to support the view that OST programs are a universal panacea for all the problems that OST proponents claim they are. Based on the few programs that have been rigorously evaluated and found effective, it is unrealistic to expect the current generation of OST programs to achieve most or even some of the outcomes articulated, such as those in California's debates on Proposition 49. Designing and implementing effective programs will take careful planning and attention. It would also likely take very significant funding.

We summarize here some basic information requirements that need to be addressed if programming is to be improved and the current debate is to become more productive:

- local assessments, using surveys and other field instruments, to clarify demand for specific services by specific classes of clients and the level and quality of existing providers
- development of forums for public consideration of the results of such analyses
- creation of more-systematic program evaluations with proper controls for self-selection and, where possible, the effect of participation levels; documentation of the impact of varying program elements or contexts; determination of the effects by age group or characteristic of participant; and attention to measuring cost effectiveness
- As there is little value to a strong evaluation of a weak intervention, these quality evaluations should be applied selectively to large, publicly funded programs and, any well-designed and funded programs with potentially wide impact (see Walker, 2004, for ideas on selection)
- dissemination of standardized measures of participation levels and intensity that are regularly reported and aggregated, combined, when possible, with serious attention to participation effects in program evaluations

- development and dissemination of tools to collect and report cost information and compiling of information necessary to undertake cost-effectiveness evaluations, with the ultimate goal of comparing OST programs to other alternative
- development, demonstration, testing, and evaluation of practical and cost-effective means to improve participant recruitment and enrollment practices for targeted services
- development of effective forums and incentives to disseminate existing standards, guidelines, and best practices as they evolve or are uncovered through research
- support for collection and analysis of data for use in decision making about provision of services, stronger monitoring, assessment, and accountability based on those guidelines and practices, including stronger incentives for performance.

Acknowledgments

The authors of this report are indebted to the many people who supported the work. First and foremost, we thank the management and staff at the Wallace Foundation for their support throughout this project. Kimberley Jinnett and Ed Pauly were especially helpful in providing critical feedback, assisting us in connecting to other very informed colleagues and practitioners in the field, and providing continued guidance and assistance.

Several research colleagues in the OST field provided us with critical comments at crucial moments, including Karen Pittman, Heather Weiss, Robert Halpern, and Jean Grossman. We thank them for their input, without which this report certainly would have suffered. In addition, we thank the reviewers of the draft for their comments that helped improve the report: Janet Currie, Robert Granger, and Robinson Hollister.

Finally, we thank our colleagues at RAND for their support in this project. Sheila Kirby acted as senior adviser to the project and greatly assisted in creating an effective organization. Others provided feedback and comments, including Becky Kilburn, Lynn Karoly, and Arie Kapetyn. In addition, we would like to thank Jennifer Wong and Heather Barney, who were instrumental in developing the review.

All errors and remaining flaws are the responsibility of the authors.

Abbreviations

AERA	American Educational Research Association
BB/BS	Big Brothers and Big Sisters
DHHS	U.S. Department of Health and Human Services
DoD	U.S. Department of Defense
DOEd	U.S. Department of Education
DOJ	U.S. Department of Justice
ESS	Extended-Service School
FY	fiscal year
GAO	U.S. General Accounting Office
IOM	Institute of Medicine
MDRC	Manpower Demonstration Research Corporation
MOST	Making the Most of Out-of-School Time
NAESP	National Association of Elementary School Principals
NHES	National Household Education Surveys
NIOST	National Institute on Out-of-School Time
NRC	National Research Council
NSACA	National School-Age Care Alliance
OST	out-of-school time
QOP	Quantum Opportunities Program
STAR	Student/Teacher Achievement Ratio
TASC	The After-School Corporation
21st CCLC	21st Century Community Learning Centers
WIA	Workforce Investment Act

CHAPTER ONE

Introduction

Significant public attention, in the press, on Web sites, and by political candidates is focused on whether and how to provide group-based programs for youth during their non-school time. Out-of-school-time (OST) programs have existed in America since at least the 1880s, and although the discussion around providing improved or more accessible programs oftentimes seems new and urgent, such concerns have been part of a decades-long debate that has ebbed and flowed with little resolution.

Group-based OST programs that offer supervision or services to youth can be found in every state and locale, some existing for decades. They include programs intended to provide a safe haven for youth who otherwise lack a supervised place to be; prevent problematic behaviors, such as drug use or pregnancy; improve academic proficiency, as with programs designed to improve test scores; and support specific hobbies and interests. While diverse in goals, structures, and delivery, historically OST service providers have had several important characteristics in common:

- Unlike schools, participation was voluntary on the part of individuals and families, and these people were responsible for searching out and accessing services.
- Supply was provided through local markets that were fragmented, loosely connected, and heterogeneous.
- Programs were supported primarily by fee-for-service or private philanthropic donations and more recently by public subsidy.

This field has grown at a rapid rate since the 1960s, and with this growth has come a resurgence of debate about the purposes of OST programming and how best to meet those purposes. While the debate is not new, some important developments might make it seem more urgent now.

Rapid growth in demand and provision, especially of school-age care services, has occurred as a result of the shift in the economy to two-income families and the growth of women with children in the workforce. Many parents now need or demand before- and after-school care for their children.

Different stakeholders and constituencies have asserted in the past, and are asserting vociferously now, ambitious and varied goals beyond school-age care for OST provision and therefore different content for programming. This can vary by the age of the participant. For example, some programs for younger children might focus on playtime and supporting basic reading and counting skills. Programs for older youth might emphasize avoidance of risky behaviors, job training, work skills, and more competitive sports. Many, including legislators, policymakers, philanthropies, and youth-advocacy groups are turning to this field to address gaps in academic and youth-development support currently left by existing institutions: families, schools, community-based organizations, and government social services. While past pushes to broaden the scope of what OST programs should accomplish have occurred, the current effort is cojoined with increased efforts at standards-based reform and accountability in the education sector that emphasizes test-score results. Thus, some advocate for OST providers to be entrusted more than ever before with the academic skill building of children and youth, potentially making the providers part of the system of public education and accountable to its goals. Others admonish against this academic emphasis and focus on providing programs where children can learn better social skills and find mentors and role models to help them deal with difficult circumstances. Yet others advocate for OST programs that allow necessary, safe playtime.

The success of different stakeholder groups in promoting the need for OST programs is apparent in the growth of publicly funded programming. For example, the federally funded 21st Century Community Learning Centers (21st CCLC), which provide after-school care to children across the United States, rose from $0 in 1994 to $1 billion annually by 2002 (and remains steady at this amount). In California, funding for the state's school-based after-school care program is projected to exceed $500 million annually by 2006–2007, about a tenfold increase since 1997. These are only two of many federal, state, city, local, and philanthropic sources of support for such programs.

Furthermore, some of these programs are now being held accountable for meeting goals derived from the source of their funding stream. For example, the 21st CCLC was developed by the U.S. Department of Education (DOEd) and others at least in part to help address student academic-achievement gaps, and its effectiveness is being measured using student test scores. Its future public funding will in part be determined by its ability to meet education goals. Such accountability was unheard of for OST programs 50 or even 20 years ago.

In short, the field is at an important, if not entirely new, point of rethinking its purposes. Current papers on Web sites, proposed legislation, journal articles, and speeches indicate disparate views about the purposes of provision, the costs and benefits of provision, the characteristics of quality programs, the level of demand, and how to improve local capacity. Different actors are searching for the mechanisms by which to engage each other in useful and productive dialogues about how to further organize the field so that it is more effective, what that means in terms of public policy, and how greater organization, coordination, or collaboration can improve the outcomes of provision.

Research Purpose and Questions

The Wallace Foundation, a supporter of programs in the OST field, is interested in supporting a well-informed and honest conversation about the need to extend OST programs and goals and about how to improve current OST provision to meet those goals, if improvement is deemed needed. While recognizing that the debate is not new, the foundation hopes to make it more effective in addressing evolving societal needs than in the past. As part of its efforts, the foundation asked the RAND Corporation to identify the major issues facing the field as it continues to grow and evolve, to access and organize the current knowledge base that can be used to address these issues, and to identify key gaps in knowledge that might help address the issue of where the field should be heading.

The purpose of this report is to systematically examine, organize, and summarize in an objective and neutral fashion the research base in the ongoing discussions about how to improve the OST field, expanding its goals and provisions simultaneously past that of basic school-age care. The report focuses on what is known about whether and how youth access OST group-based programs that attempt to meet goals other than child care, how participation in these programs contribute to a broad array of youth outcomes, and ways that providers, communities, and decision makers can increase the benefits of OST programs. In particular we have identified and assessed the evidence with respect to five key issues within the ongoing debate:

- the level of unmet demand
- the state of knowledge about the types of outcomes that participation in OST programs are expected to impact and the nature of the impacts observed
- determinants of quality in program offerings
- determinants of participation and selection
- practices effective in ensuring that quality programming is available to meet local demand.

We have carefully limited the scope of this inquiry. The subject of this examination is the set of group-based programs for school-age (approximately 6–18) children and adolescents offered by community organizations outside the home, such as Boys and Girls Clubs, YMCAs and YWCAs, parks and recreation departments, after-school programs, libraries, and museums. We use the term *OST programs* to capture our focus on the hours before and after school as well as during the summer. Because much of the literature focuses solely on after-school programs during the school year, the reader will also see this term used.

The current debate is being fueled in large part by the growth in public and philanthropic support for such programs; therefore, this report focuses on publicly provided programs that are usually at least partially subsidized. We do not focus on private or fee-based programs (such as piano lessons, or private school-age care), extracurricular activities that are school-based and school- or parent-funded (e.g., school sports teams and interests clubs), nor one-on-one programs involving only mentoring and tutoring or case management approaches (e.g., Quantum Opportunities Program [QOP]). Although the latter type of program is often subsidized (such as Big Brothers and Big Sisters [BB/BS]), the effectiveness of such resource and staff/volunteer-intensive approaches has been well documented, most recently in *Community Programs to Promote Youth Development* (National Research Council [NRC] and Institute of Medicine [IOM], 2002). We do not include activities that children participate in within the home—for example, watching TV, reading, or doing homework—nor do we include the free play that children undertake within their homes or neighborhoods.

The audience for this report is those active in improving OST services. This includes service providers, advocates, philanthropists, and policymakers. It can be used as a reference for them on the issues within the debate and the current state of knowledge, and the evidence base for that knowledge, on OST issues.

Methods and Caveats

This report documents a literature review. We carefully reviewed the existing literature and provide synopses of it in an organized and objective fashion to address the above five issues. This should prove a different approach from much of the existing literature that is advocacy-based. As a review of existing literature, we do not necessarily provide new information or new insights for those very familiar with the field. Rather, the objective was to advance the dialogue among stakeholders by identifying major questions, assessing the evidence concerning those questions, and identifying gaps in the evidence.

An important purpose of a literature review is to weigh the relative scientific rigor of the evidence and draw conclusions from the most objective evidence. A major issue facing us in undertaking the review was what literature to include, not so much by subject areas, which were determined by the issues addressed and our definitions above, but by rigor. In this review we were faced with several realities that determined how we selected literature.

First, many areas of possible interest have not actually been the subject of empirical exploration. For example, investigating the issue of demand revealed many assertions, but few empirically based studies (surveys or historical data analysis) of current or projected demand. Second, some of the issue areas we identified were amenable to using a gold-standard design (random assignment, experimental), such as the issue of program effects. For other issue areas—for example, the level of demand—other types of methods, such as surveys and analysis of historical demand and supply data, were appropriate. Third, within an issue area, the studies uncovered varied tremendously in the analytic rigor appropriate for the issue at hand. For example, in program evaluation where an experimental design would be preferred for drawing inferences, many studies did not meet this standard of rigor, thus limiting causal inferences.

We therefore chose a flexible, issue-area-by-issue-area approach to selecting literature to review. We attempted to apply a simple rule—to use the literature that was the most rigorous for that particular issue area. Each chapter contains information about the literature reviewed and the nature and rigor of the evidence; the "Sources and Approach" box provides some more details. In concluding sections of each chapter we caveat the findings appropriately. In this way we can both indicate what the level of rigor in the field is on that issue as well as point to how the rigor of empirical evidence could be improved. We provide caveats about study limitations and make recommendations about how to improve the knowledge base on that particular issue.

Lastly, but perhaps most importantly, answers to the questions posed will come from value judgments as much as from empirical evidence. In short, whether this country provides further support for more ambitious goals and universal provision of high-quality services will depend on the value placed by the majority on those services, considering other uses of funds. For example, what these programs should be doing is value-laden and not subject to empirical investigation. However, value judgments can be informed by objective evidence about what parents want for their children, what children and youth seek in OST programs, what current programs attempt to accomplish, whether they have been successful in achieving their goals, and at what cost. This literature review is intended to help inform the debate with a clear view of the empirical evidence, but equally will point out areas were evidence is scant or unavailable or where empiricism cannot fully address essential questions.

Sources and Approach

We searched databases for 1985 through September 2003, with selective updates from the latter date. Examples of search terms include *after school care, informal learning,* and *out of school time.* The sources were

- biographical databases, including ERIC, Ed Abstracts, Social Sciences Citation Index, and Social Sciences Abstract
- Web sites, such as the Harvard Family Evaluation Exchange, National Institute on Out-of-School-Time (NIOST), After-school Alliance, and Public/Private Ventures
- expert recommendations from within RAND and experts in the field, especially consulting experts for the Wallace Foundation.

This provided source material from highly specified program evaluations to historical analysis to theoretical arguments. We classified each piece according to the following scheme:

- *Scholarly.* We rated peer-reviewed documents as more rigorous than non-peer-reviewed ones.
- *Evidentiary base.* We rated the evidentiary base for the conclusions drawn in the document, based on what was appropriate. For example, program evaluations are amenable to random-assignment experiments. For program evaluations in Chapter Four, we char-

---

acterized studies using those designs as more rigorous. However, measuring demand and support for public programming is better assessed through statistical analysis of survey or historical data. In Chapter Three, we therefore reviewed these types of studies. The following ranking from most to least rigorous applies to program evaluations, program-quality determinants, and to some aspects of assessing mechanisms for increasing participation:

- experimental, with random controlled trial
- quasi-experimental, with comparison groups
- statistical controls of descriptive data, including surveys
- qualitative comparative cases
- anecdotal evidence

    • single case studies
    • expert panels
    • single experts/principles
    • other

• *Efficiency.* To maximize efficiency, we drew when possible from recent syntheses and review literature following publication of the synthesis source for any major modifications or additions in the field.

We attempted to use as much as possible the more rigorous peer-reviewed literature, however, in many cases, given the level of research available, we use less rigorous literature. We caveat conclusions appropriately.

Organization of Report

This report has seven substantive chapters. Chapter Two provides a historical review of the OST field and the current policy issues. Chapter Three describes what is known about levels of demand for OST services. Chapter Four presents the evidence on what types of outcomes have been associated with OST programs and factors associated with level or types of outcomes. Chapter Five reviews the literature on specific program factors—such as the stability of staff, whether the program content is age-appropriate, and staff training—that some analysts have tried to link to outcomes. Chapter Six reviews the evidence for how to effectively recruit and retain participants. Chapter Seven assesses the literature on practices effective in building capacity. Chapter Eight summarizes the literature findings, draws out policy issues, and directs the reader's attention to further research that could be productively undertaken to improve the knowledge base in this field.

CHAPTER TWO

Historical Context

OST programs have a long tradition in the United States, dating back at least to the 1880s. Although it might seem that how children and youth spend their nonschool time is more of a public policy debate that ever before, in reality concern about OST programming has waxed and waned for decades. In this chapter we provide the context for current calls for change by summarizing the history of this field and providing the present context. In doing so, we have relied heavily on the work of Robert Halpern, who has written extensively about the progression and history of this field. Our contribution is to update his work with a more current view of the field and to show how this field is now being considered as part of a broad public-policy debate on public support for group-based programs.

The chapter reviews the phases of development of OST programming in the United States, noting important changes that have taken place. It then describes the current scene and provides information about different important actors in the field. It summarizes the current debate and the questions posed.

In general, it shows that while the field has grown and changed over time, the goals of OST programming have always been complex and debatable. The primary difference between the field historically and now is the growth in provision and in government support.

Early Phases of Development

The field of OST care has progressed through several different phases since its birth in early philanthropic efforts to help immigrant families in our urban centers.

Through the 1920s

In the second half of the 19th century (1865–1900), significant numbers of immigrants reached the shores of America and settled into urban centers. Often ill equipped to immediately prosper due to a combination of little wealth, skills unmatched to the urban economy, and lack of English-language proficiency, immigrants in several successive waves found assistance from philanthropic settlement houses. In these centers children of immigrants were taught English skills and provided with minimum health-care services and some limited food and clothing. Attendance at or entry into these services was voluntary, with the services usually being offered through philanthropic donations and the work of largely middle-class volunteers.

The latter quarter of the century began to see a significant shift in the focus of such settlements due to major changes that continued until approximately the 1940s. First, states began passing restrictive child-labor laws that prevented what had been significant employment of young children. Second, more communities began encouraging, or mandating, that children attend school through elementary grades. As the decades passed the mandates eventually covered middle grades and finally high school, significantly increasing the percentage of children enrolled in school and the number of days they attended. The impacts on enrollments are clear from the National Center on Educational Statistics (Snyder, 1993).

- Enrollment in school increased throughout these decades, not so much due to population growth rates, but due to increasing numbers of children entering and continuing through high school. For example, in 1879–1880 total enrollments in public schools equaled 9,757,000. By 1929–1930 this had more than doubled, to 25,678,000.

- In 1889–1890 approximately 77 percent of children ages 5–17 were enrolled in school, but few attended high school. About 11 percent of 14–17-year-olds attended high school by 1899–1900. By 1929–30, this had increased to 51 percent.
- The average number of days spent in school in 1879–1880 was 81; by 1929–1930 this had increased to 143 days.

The nature of the settlement houses shifted in this time period. With more and more children attending schools, the philanthropic community began to provide charitable child-care provision for the working-class poor for nonschool hours when their parents were still at work or working from home on the production of piece-rate products. According to Halpern (2002), many of these programs were intended primarily as a refuge for the children and a diversion from the dangers of the streets. Typically one would open in a storefront or church and expand over time as more participants engaged. All children were welcome, and activities could include anything from supervised play to formal music clubs to organized sports and tutoring. It is in this period of time that "boys and girls clubs" were founded and began to grow.

In the first two decades of the twentieth century, as Halpern notes, the field "took on the decentralized, idiosyncratic form that would characterize it throughout the century. Different kinds of agencies sponsored after-school programs and each local sponsor set its policies and priorities. The role and importance of specific providers varied from city to city. After-school programs emerged, as they would remain, mostly privately sponsored and funded" (2002, p. 183). Figure 2.1 provides a schematic of the decentralized system that developed during this period. We note that under this paradigm program effectiveness was assumed, and evaluation of provider services was not a part of the culture.

Even in this early time period the purposes of the services were debated, but primarily among the private providers or funders. Minimally, the centers provided a safe haven for youth, often combined with some health checks. But over these decades, other goals began to be espoused as the nascent social sciences began to grow and inform sponsors and providers. Some argued for unstructured playtime

Figure 2.1
Local Markets with Numerous Providers

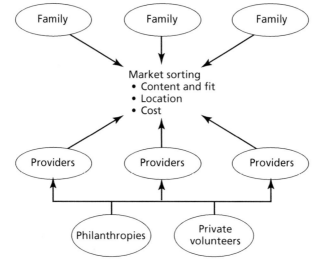

and some for more structured playtime, recognizing the importance of these activities to cognitive and social development. Others saw an opportunity to further the Americanization of immigrant youth or to provide basic tutoring services. Still others sought to reinforce the social norms of the time or provide vocational skills, especially to older male youth. These goals were debated and discussed over time, with no model gaining ascendancy and considerable variation in the activities demanded by families and provided within locales by individual providers.

From 1930 to 1950

During this time the purposes and structure of the field changed little. Two major events, the Great Depression and World War II, did have an impact.

The Great Depression had two effects. First, as the inevitable budget cuts in public education forced schools to drop electives, settlements, clubs, and churches attempted to provide compensating programs. Second, and perhaps more importantly, these privately provided services also attempted to compensate for the growing deficits in food, clothing, health, and familial attention that accompanied the large-scale unemployment of the times.

It marked the first time federal funds were used to support child-care services. According to Halpern, "a modest proportion of New Deal funds and resources became available to programs, primarily through the Works Progress Administration (WPA), the Federal Arts Projects, and the National Youth Administration (NYA)" (2002, p. 194).

Entry into World War II saw another temporary phenomenon. Fathers left the home to fight overseas, and women workers entered into the war effort. For the first time, people began to recognize the phenomena of the "latch-key" child. This resulted in many OST programs taking on a straightforward child-care function. Local governments set up Defense Day Care facilities and Defense Recreation Committees to help keep children productively occupied while their fathers and mothers supported the war effort. Schools stayed open late to provide extended-care programs. The federal role, however, remained minimal, in part because of concerns over supporting maternal neglect of children.

As the war ended and the economy began to return to normal, the governmental support for these services waned, and the field returned largely to private philanthropic suppliers and volunteers. As before, provider effectiveness was assumed as long as children were safe and in healthy environments, a judgment made by the parents.

From 1950 to 1970

The decades following World War II saw several changes that again impacted the nature of service provision. Most importantly, some neighborhoods in the inner cities began to change, being perceived as more dangerous than in the past, with the growth of youth alienation, intergenerational poverty, drug abuse, and violent crime. These changes were accompanied by public policy to address the "urban blight" that faced our cities, including the War on Poverty programs of the Johnson administration.

This climate encouraged a rethinking of the role of OST programs, focusing attention on provision of a safe haven for youth, programs geared toward prevention of violent or criminal activities and more productive youth development. Aided by growing research on youth development, the field began to establish activities geared toward educational enrichment, while providers struggled to obtain funding from some of the federal sources available, such as Title I funds for compensatory education or the Youth Corp.

From 1970 to 2000

The last several decades have seen significant social and economic changes that have encouraged the spread of child-care providers and greater pressure on providers to improve program content.

Growth in demand and supply. In the last three decades a series of factors combined to produce growing demand for child-care services in general and OST services specifically and greatly expanded private provision. First and foremost, shifts in the economy, in family bread-winner patterns, and in the education of women brought more women into the labor market, including women with school-age children. According to the *Statistical Abstract of the United States* (U.S. Census Bureau, 2003), in 1970, approximately 21 percent of women with children under the age of 18 worked. By 2002, approximately 73 percent worked. By 2002, 65 percent of women with children under the age of 6 worked, and 79 percent of women with children between the ages of 6 and 17 worked. This represents 67.4 million children under 18 years of age with working mothers (Costello, Wight, and Stone, 2003).

Women entering the workforce in record numbers resulted in a significant growth in child-care services. Based on figures from Casper and O'Connell (1998) and O'Neill and O'Connell (2001) the total number of child-care establishments with payrolls rose from 24,813 in 1977 to 62,054 20 years later. According to Goodman (1995), employment in the child-day-care services industry grew from 145,500 in 1972 to 501,900 in 1994, the latest year for available data.

Many of these services had been largely provided on a fee-for-service basis and can be described as a free-market function with parents searching out the best OST options for them and their children. There has been concern, however, over the plight of the children of the working-class poor or of the indigent. Without access to resources, they might lack the before and after care bought with fees by the more well-to-do. Blau and Currie (2003) indicate, however, that low-income families will still choose to work, but opt for lower-cost child-care options. Federal, state, and local programs have developed to minimally provide child-care services for low-income families.

Recent findings fueling interest in OST programming. More clearly than in the past, research findings, usually of a descriptive or correlation nature, fueled demand for OST programs that provide more than child care. Three strands of work have had particular impact and have often been cited by advocates to build public support for changes in programming.

- Studies tracking crime rates for youth indicated a spike in the number of youth arrested or who were victims of crime in the hours immediately after school, especially between 3 and 6 P.M. on school days and 8 and 10 P.M. on nonschool days. These findings galvanized some parents and providers to advocate for after-school and weekend evening activities for children. For example, Fight Crime: Invest in Children was formed to represent police groups and crime victims to promote after-school care programs as a way to reduce crime in communities. A joint DOEd and U.S. Department of Justice (DOJ) report quotes then Vice President Gore as saying, "This period of time between the school bell and the factory whistle is a most vulnerable time for children. These are the hours when children are more likely to engage in at-risk behavior and are more vulnerable to the dangers that still exist in too many neighborhoods and communities" (2000, p. 8). Duffett and Johnson (2004), in a survey of youth in middle- and high-school grades, found that youth agree. Seventy-seven percent of the youth surveyed agreed that "a lot of kids get into trouble when they're bored and have nothing to do." Eighty-five percent agreed that kids who participate in organized activities such as a team or a club after school are "better off" than those who have a lot of time to themselves.
- Youth-development experts drew attention to behavioral studies that suggested that children and youth need trusting relationships between the youth and adults to become productively engaged. Reports cited by the joint DOEd and DOJ study (2000) noted the

positive impact of youth programs on preventing risky behaviors. For example, the report stated, "Youth ages 10–16, who have a relationship with a mentor, are 46 percent less likely to start using drugs, 27 percent less likely to start drinking alcohol, and 33 percent less likely to participate in violent activity" (p. 12).[1]

- Studies of children from poverty backgrounds increasingly emphasized the important role early and continued exposure to enriched environments had on levels of academic achievement. Numerous studies of differences in student achievement by groups (see, for example, the summary of studies in Grissmer et al., 2000) indicated that while significant differences in achievement exists, other research indicated that some schools and some OST programs might be effectively used to improve student achievement, attitudes, and motivations toward school and achievement. This led to a growing insistence that children, especially from low-income families, needed continuing support throughout their youth to be able to compete effectively in the adult job market. These concerns have led to calls for greater public support for OST programs geared toward academic achievement or that provide culturally enriching experiences for low-income youth.

This emphasis on academic achievement further increased as a result of what has become known as the standards-based accountability movement. Throughout the late 1980s to the present, states have used test results to hold schools and students accountable. In January 2002, President Bush signed the federal No Child Left Behind Act, which held schools responsible for the performance of all students. While not directly supporting better OST programming, this legislation coupled with state moves in the same direction of accountability has increased interest in supplemental programming during OST for children at risk of failure.

Added together, these trends and research findings have helped create a different market for OST programming than existed in the past.

---

[1] For this finding, the report cites Joseph Tierney and Jean Grossman, with Nancy Resch, *Making a Difference: An Impact Study of Big Brothers–Big Sisters,* Philadelphia: Public/Private Ventures, 1995.

First, the need for child care has expanded greatly. Second, the nature and quality of that care has become increasingly important to many families and to the public. Finally, the emphasis on safe places for children to play of the past has turned into calls for "providing supervision, offering enriching experiences and positive social interactions, and improving academic achievement" (DOEd and DOJ, 2000, p. 7).

Growth in federal role. At the same time, the federal role in OST provision grew, largely indirectly, based on three arguments. First, government has been concerned with reducing the social inequities in our society. One of the most pernicious is the achievement gap associated with racial, ethnic, and income characteristics of families. Different programs, such as Head Start and Title 1, were instituted to reduce this gap. The latter has supported after-school-service provision during this time; schools began to use Title 1 compensatory education funds for the provision of after-school care for students from low-income families. These programs necessarily had some components to improve the academic understanding of participants, and were not solely for child care.

Second, another rationale has been to support working families to encourage a strong economy and prevent families from having to access more expensive government subsidies, such as welfare. Thus, the federal government passed legislation providing a child-care tax credit. Support for working families has been integrated with efforts to decrease inequities in several instances. For example, the U.S. Department of Health and Human Services (DHHS) encourages the provision of child-care services through several different programs geared toward low-income families.

Third, the market for service provision might not function well—for example, there might be failures in the information flow needed for parents to effectively place their children. Thus, the government also supports some more limited programs that provide for referral services.

Current Scene

Demand for services has grown dramatically, but, according to Blau and Currie (2003), school-age care arrangements vary considerably. Approximately 73 percent of children age 5–14 with working mothers are cared for by a parent or relative, while about 17 percent are in organized activities such as after-school programs. But even mothers who are not employed use these services; approximately 11 percent of children of nonworking mothers attend some sort of formal organization other than school. This also varies by the age of the child, with the greatest demand for services being for younger children. At age five, 27 percent of children of working mothers are in organized activities outside the home. By age 14, this drops to 13 percent.

Meanwhile school-age children still spend significant time in unsupervised care (Blau and Currie, 2003). In 1999, 10.5 percent of children age 5–14 of employed mothers were in unsupervised self-care for part of the day. Among nine-year-olds with working mothers, about 8 percent are sometimes unsupervised. By 14 years of age, nearly half (45 percent) are sometimes unsupervised. Contrary to what some might believe, the probability of being unsupervised is greater with increasing income and for whites; it is lower for Hispanics and blacks. These findings were underscored by a recent survey from Public Agenda (Duffett and Johnson, 2004). This survey of middle-school and high-school youth found that 28 percent reported being home alone after school at least three out of five days in a typical school week.

U.S. Census Bureau (Lugaila, 2003) data provide a more detailed picture of children in extracurricular activities, including clubs, sports, and lessons. Nationally in 2000, 59 percent of children 6–17 years of age (28.4 million) participated in at least one of the three activities. Older children were more likely to participate in sports than younger children (31 percent of 6–11-year-olds, compared to 37 percent of 12–17-year-olds). Participation in clubs did not vary by age, with about 34 percent in each age bracket participating. From 1994 to 2000, participation in sports declined overall (e.g., from 42 percent for 12–17-year-olds to 37 percent) and participation in clubs declined overall (e.g., from 43 percent for 12–17-year-olds to 34 percent). Participation in lessons increased for the same age group from 19 percent to 26 percent.

Meanwhile advocacy groups and other actors remain intensely involved in development of programs and services. Figure 2.2 provides a schematic of the different actors now involved and the roles they play. Even with these changes, the following still hold:

Figure 2.2
Current Scene

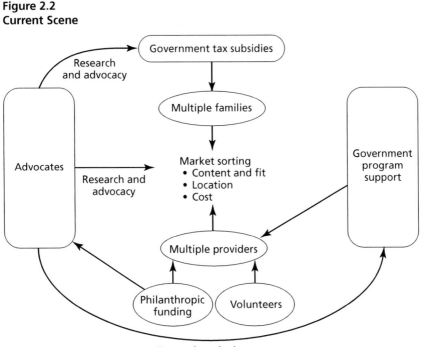

RAND *MG264-2.2*

- Unlike schools, participation remains voluntary on the part of individuals and families, and these individuals search for the services that they need and can afford or are aided in doing so by government programs.
- Supply is still provided through undeveloped local markets, described as fragmented, loosely coupled, and heterogeneous (Halpern, 2002).
- The market is imperfect, at least in the sense that information about programs is not always well publicized or available to parents and access to affordable programs is not always available locally (Blau and Currie, 2003).
- Programs are supported primarily by fee-for-service, private philanthropic donations, or subsidies for the poor. Subsidization is

justified by economic or equity concerns, and the majority of parents are still primarily responsible for finding and paying for programs.

Changing Actors and Roles

New actors have entered into this scene and are beginning to dramatically affect the nature of the marketplace for OST as well as the level of governmental support provided. In the past, OST was the province of a few philanthropists and volunteers aided by relatively weak social-science research. Political activity and supporting infrastructure has grown dramatically.

Growing government role. The federal government has become increasingly involved in the financial support of providers as well as through subsidies for child-care services. Table 2.1 provides a synopsis of some of the relevant federal programs now in place. Many do not have provision of OST as the primary focus; however, funds can be used for these purposes. Perhaps most important is the tax credit for child-care services that goes directly to families. Other programs tend to provide funding to provider organizations rather than families. The Finance Project (Padgette, 2003) estimated that in fiscal year (FY) 2001 the federal government invested $3.6 billion in OST services, not including the foregone taxes from the credit. With that investment came specific accountability that had not been a part of the field before.

In a significant change from the past, the federal government began to directly support after-school programs with the creation of the 21st CCLC program in 1994. This program provided funds for the operations of centers throughout the country, primarily for children from low-income families. While the content of the programs is unspecified, they were expected to increase student academic achievement.

States have also been actively pushing their support and involvement in the provision of after-school services. For example, the state of California has moved toward significant state funding of after-school programs. Proposition 49 asked California voters to support more universal coverage for after-school care programs, asserting that such programs could reduce crime, improve grades and test scores, reduce course repetition, reduce school drop-out, and reduce the need for remedial education (Attorney General of California, 2002).

Table 2.1
Federal Programs and Roles

Internal Revenue Service

Child and Dependent Care Tax Credit—Credit for 20 percent to 30 percent of qualified child-care expenses for children under 13 or with special needs.

Employer-Provided Dependent Care Benefit Tax Deduction—Employees may exclude up to $5,000 of employer-provided benefits from taxable income and can include the costs of employer-provided day-care center or other payments for child care.

U.S. Department of Education

Title I—This long-standing compensatory education funding stream goes to schools, though the states, to support achievement of low-income students. Funds can be used in a variety of ways, including for after-school programs.

21st CCLC—Funds are provided through the states to schools that might contract with community-based organizations or private and public organizations to provide after-school programming to students from schools that serve primarily Title I students. Programs are to advance academic achievement.

Gear-Up—Grants are provide on a competitive basis to districts and schools to increase college readiness. After-school programs have been funded.

Department of Health and Human Services

Administration for Children and Families—This agency is responsible for federal programs that promote the economic and social well-being of families, children, individuals, and communities. It oversees the **Child Care Bureau**, which supports low-income working families through child-care financial assistance. The Child Care Bureau oversees the **Child Care and Development Fund** and has contracted for technical assistance to providers through the **Finance Project**. It also supports research on emerging trends in child care.

Child Care and Development Fund—Funds are given to providers of child services, including schools, community-based organizations, and public and private organizations, to help low-income families with children up to age 12. Programs can provide contracted child-care slots or vouchers to families.

Temporary Assistance to Needy Families—Funds are provided to needy families with children to promote job preparation and work, reduce out-of-wedlock pregnancies, and encourage formation of two-parent families. States have flexibility on use of funds and have used them for child-care services.

National Institute for Child Health and Development—This institute provides research into child development and has been instrumental in forwarding the knowledge foundation of the needs of children for healthy growth.

Table 2.1 (continued)

Department of Labor

Workforce Investment Act (WIA)—The department oversees WIA, which creates councils to assess local youth-development needs and services and make recommendations to local workforce boards. The boards received Youth Formula Grants that can be used to support OST provision.

Joint (Departments of Justice, Health and Human Services, and Education)

Safe Schools/Healthy Students Initiative—Grants are provided to promote healthy development and prevent violent behavior through after-school activities.

Department of Housing and Urban Development

Youthbuild—Grants are provided on a competitive basis to nonprofit organizations to assist high-risk dropouts ages 16–24 to learn housing-construction job skills and to complete their high-school education.

In November 2002, California voters passed Proposition 49, the After School Education and Safety Program Act, by a 56.6 percent approval. The act expands the existing Before and After School Learning and Safe Neighborhood Partnerships Program by providing grants to elementary and middle schools for after-school programs such that: (1) all existing programs will be continued, (2) eventually every public school will be eligible for funding, and (3) increases in funding will be targeted to schools with a poverty level of 50 percent or greater. Funding for the programs will be dependent on growth in the state revenues.

Other states have jumped on this bandwagon. In New Jersey, the After 3 Initiative sponsored by Governor McGreevey was launched in 2004. The program will utilize a $15 million investment to create a public-private partnership to bring educational and recreational after-school programs to 20,000 children. It will be administered by a nonprofit organization. In South Dakota, Governor Janklow signed a bill that provides $1 million in grants to OST programs in the state.

National advocacy groups and intermediaries. With the growing population of families needing support, the growing research base on some of the issues concerning OST, and the growth in Web-based advocacy and dissemination of research, it is no surprise that a number of private nonprofit advocacy groups have sprouted up along with local intermediaries intending to help support quality service provision. A growing network of formal organizations that dedicate considerable resources to improving OST programming now exists. They provide an array of resources, including research, information, technical assistance, and advocacy focused on improving and expanding the offerings in the market place. The major national organizations are briefly described in Table 2.2, but include only a small fraction of the many organizations now functioning.

Table 2.2
National Research and Advocacy Groups

Afterschool Alliance was founded as an outgrowth of the 21st CCLC Initiative of DOEd and the Mott Foundation. It is dedicated to raising awareness of the importance of after-school programs and advocating for quality, affordable programs for all children. It is supported by public, private, and nonprofit organizations that share the vision of ensuring that all children have access to after-school programs by 2010. (http://www.afterschoolalliance.org/)

Fight Crime: Invest in Kids, founded in 1996, is a nonprofit anticrime organization of police organizations and crime victims. Its mission is to identify strategies for youth-crime prevention and interventions, including early care and education programs and putting that information in the hands of policymakers and the public. (http://www.fightcrime.org/)

Finance Project, with support from several foundations and the U.S. Child Care Bureau, developed technical assistance resources to assist state and community leaders to develop financial resources to support quality programming. (http://www.financeprojectinfo.org/OST/default.asp)

Forum for Youth Investment, formed in 1998, provides a platform for discussion of investments in youth development for those in the allied youth fields. It provides research and analysis, communication and dissemination of results, technical assistance, network access, and implementation assistance. (http://www.forumforyouthinvestment.org/)

Harvard Family Research Project, founded in 1983 at the Harvard Graduate School of Education, strives to increase the effectiveness of public and private organizations and communities as they promote child development, student achievement, healthy family functioning, and community development. It collects, analyzes, synthesizes, and disseminates information to guide problem solving and decision making. (http://www.gse.harvard.edu/hfrp/)

Table 2.2 (continued)

National Conference of State Legislatures, with the help of the Charles Stewart Mott Foundation, developed the Afterschool Project of the Learn, Work, and Earn Program at the conference. It provides information and technical assistance to state lawmakers on after-school programs. (http://www.ncls.org/programs/cyf/afterdesc.htm)

National Governors Association developed the Center for Best Practices that supports governors and other state leaders in sharing and creating effective practices intended to expand and enhance extra learning opportunities for youth. In addition, it is providing 13 states with $10,000 grants to conduct state summits on extra learning opportunities. (http://www.nga.org/center/topics/1,1188,D_363,00.html)

National Institute on Out-of-School Time, in association with Wellesley Centers for Women, has a mission to ensure that all children, youth, and families have access to high-quality programs, activities, and opportunities during nonschool hours. It has helped develop standards for provision. (http://www.niost.org/)

National League of Cities launched the Institute for Youth, Education, and Families to recognize and promote the unique roles that city and local leaders play in strengthening families and improving outcomes for children and youth. Its projects include increasing the availability and improving the quality of expanded learning opportunities for children and youth and helping municipal leaders view after-school programs as an essential resource in efforts to raise academic achievement among students in their communities. (http://www.nlc.org/)

National Parent Teachers Association formed a partnership with the Charles Stewart Mott Foundation to promote after-school programs. It offers resources to help schools, principals, teachers, and parents develop or assess programs through a program called Doors Open After School. (http://www.pta.org/parentinvolvement/afterschool/index.asp)

National School-Age Care Alliance's (NSACA) mission is to build a profession that develops, supports, and promotes quality after-school programs for children and youth. A national membership organization with over 8,000 providers members, it has helped develop service standards and provides professional development for providers. (http://www.nsaca.org/)

U.S Conference of Mayors has developed a Best Practices Center. A recent publication, *The Partnership for Working Families: Successful City Initiatives* (June 2003), offers examples of practices currently being used in different cities throughout the country.

While one might hope that these organizations jointly provide a clearer agenda for improvements in the field, in fact they often specialize in certain areas and do not always work together. For example, NIOST has focused on the development of standards for providers, while the Afterschool Alliance advocates for universal access to quality services.

National Foundations. Foundations have been major funders of OST programs. Initially they underwrote the operations of providers to assist the poor in gaining access to services. More recently they have broadened their work. A few examples include funding for

- research on program effectiveness, including the support for the 21st CLCC evaluation by the Charles Stewart Mott foundation, research supported by the W. T. Grant Foundation on program effectiveness and how program characteristics relate to youth outcomes, and guidelines for creating successful programs developed by funding from the Wallace Foundation for evaluations of its Making the Most of Out-of-School Time (MOST) and the Extended-Service School (ESS) programs
- development of community-wide strategies for provision of services supported by national foundations in specific locales, such as the Wallace Foundation's support of efforts in Providence, Rhode Island; support in Boston by the Barr Foundation and the Boston Foundation; or support by the Robert Wood Johnson Foundation to five cities
- development and adoption of best business practices supported by the Edna McConnell Clark Foundation under its Institution and Field Building Initiative
- development of networks and intermediaries, such as the projects funded by the Charles Steward Mott Foundation that have supported the development of the Finance Project, the 21st CCLC, and the Afterschool Alliance.

The Debate

With the growth in public funding for services and calls by some advocates for more public funding comes a traditional emphasis by government for accountability of public funds. But formal accountability had not been the norm in the OST marketplace.

Few OST programs were ever evaluated and even fewer evaluated well. For example, the provision of child-care services requires only that the provider keep the children in a safe and healthy environment. But a program whose goal is to increase the number of children who are in a supervised setting needs to demonstrate that the program does increase the number of children in supervised care over the number that would have occurred without the program. Remarkably, this impact has been measured in only one rigorous evaluation, as will be discussed in Chapter Four. In contrast, the goal of an enriched environment is usually so vague in practice as to be not readily evaluated. Indeed, for programs targeted toward disadvantaged youth, prejudice on the part of the provider might have prevented serious evaluation. They would naturally assume that the services they provided were better, greater, or in some other way an improvement over what the youth would have obtained absent the services.

But now providers are increasingly taking public funds for specific purposes, such as educational achievement, and not surprisingly are expected to be able to show that the funds are properly and effectively used. Because promotion of educational achievement is a required objective of some of the major funding streams that OST providers tap into, the field can expect to see more evaluations assessing educational impacts. In 2003, however, the first large-scale evaluation of a federally supported OST program with educational objectives did not show clear positive results.

The 21st CCLC. In 1994, Congress authorized the 21st CCLC to open up schools for broader use by their communities (DOEd, 2003). In 1998 the program was refocused to provide school-based academic and recreational activities during nonschool hours and quickly grew in the U.S. budget from $40 million in FY 1998 to $1 billion in FY 2002. Grants made after April 1998 required the after-school programs to provide an academic component. In 2003 the program operated in 7,500 rural and inner city schools in 1,400 communities.

In cooperation with the Charles Stewart Mott Foundation, DOEd funded an evaluation of the program carried out by Mathematica Policy Research. Because it was the first large-scale evaluation of a national after-school program that used an experimental design, the field turned to it to confirm the important impacts that many assumed other programs were having.

In 2003, the first-year results were widely released to the national media, with galvanizing effect. The study indicated that "while 21st Century after-school centers changed where and with whom students spent some of their after-school time and increased parental involvement, they had limited influence on academic performance, no influence on feelings of safety or the number of 'latchkey' children and some negative influences on behavior" (DOEd, 2003, p. xii).

While the study was criticized on many counts and did represent only first-year data, the findings cast doubt on the legitimacy of the claims being made about the effectiveness of OST activities and forced the field into a conversation about the latent issues of reasonable goals, effectiveness, need, and evidence that had not been adequately addressed in the past (Dynarski, 2003; Weiss and Little, 2003). The second-year findings just released showed similar results (Dynarski et al., 2004).

Current discussions. At this point in time the provision of school-age care and other OST services appears to be expanding. But it is not a given that any service provision is beneficial or that public funding should be used to directly support provision.

Some advocacy groups, like the Afterschool Alliance, argue for more public funding in the existing OST market. Others see much more fundamental issues that need to be considered. In reflections and reviews of the youth-development field (a major stakeholder group in the OST debate), several authors have called for a complete review of how we promote and serve child- and youth-development in its entirety, including schooling (Connell, Gambone, and Smith, 2000; Pittman, Irby, and Ferber, 2000). These authors assert that policymakers and the public have failed to resolve how to better support positive youth development in the past because those who put forward arguments for change were poorly prepared. These authors state that past arguments were too vague, the justifications for change were weak, the stated purposes for changing were not compelling, and the chosen means were insufficient (Pittman, Irby, and Ferber, 2000, pp. 30–31).

The major issues under debate in the field that we identified, and that we seek to explore in this report, are the following:

- the level of unmet demand
- the state of knowledge about the types of outcomes that participation in OST programs are expected to impact and the nature of the impacts observed
- determinants of quality in program offerings, including what can be controlled by providers and what cannot
- determinants of participation and selection
- effective practices to ensure that adequate quality programming is available to meet the demand.

Implications

The demand for OST services has increased dramatically over time, and with the increased demand has come concerns and sometimes calls for increased quality of services to meet the needs of today's youth. These arguments have been evident in the field for some time. They have, however, grown in intensity and in the public's awareness. Parents have been supported by a growing government role in providing services. Emerging interest groups are arguing for more ambitious goals and services, and observers are calling for a rethinking of how we as a nation support families in developing productive journeys to adulthood.

A large part of the growth is based on stakeholder groups persuading public policymakers that OST programs can meet several important needs salient to many Americans: the need for supervised care for school-age children, the need to promote positive child- and youth-development outcomes, and the need to improve student performance. Because OST programs have become a matter of public policy by virtue of the use of public funds, it is important that the debates within the field be clearly elucidated and the evidence related to these debates assessed. It is for this reason that the Wallace Foundation approached RAND asking for an objective look at the literature in order to support realistic and evidence-based public policy.

CHAPTER THREE

Unmet Demand for Out-of-School-Time Services

The level of unmet demand for services, or lack of supply of quality services, has become a subject of debate because of claims, especially among after-school-program advocates, that many children go without services, much less high-quality services. Many proponents of OST programs claim that the demand for OST programs outstrips the supply of such programs by a factor of two to one. (See, for example, DOEd and DOJ, 2000.) The Afterschool Alliance (2004), a nonprofit national advocacy organization for after-school programs, has a stated goal of "ensuring that all children have access to afterschool programs by 2010."

If there is significant pent-up demand or if goals for universal provision are justified by strong positive impacts, then it makes sense to push for building increased supply and encouraging participation. However, if the opposite is true—that supply outstrips demand or that demand is suppressed because that supply is of poor quality—then ramping up the number of OST slots available would be unjustified. Instead, the focus might be on increasing the participation in existing programs shown to produce useful results. Alternatively, current supply might be more than enough for the types and levels of services now being demanded. Demand might increase if better services at affordable prices were the norm. In this case, increasing slots in high-quality programs might be considered.

In this chapter we review the very limited data available on pent-up demand and/or lack of supply. We review the evidence by type of method: surveys or polls, assumption-based calculations, program-level enrollment data, and program-level attendance data. For the most part the first two categories are found in non-peer-reviewed literature, while the latter often comes from evaluations in peer-reviewed sources. We conclude that the evidence fails to substantiate claims of pent-up demand or to provide evidence to distinguish among the conditions above. The evidence base in the published literature is simply too weak to draw any conclusions. We draw attention to the need for local-level assessments of supply and demand, especially assessing the types of services needed and demanded in local areas.

Findings from Surveys or Polls

At least some of the evidence for claims of unmet demand comes from responses to surveys or polling usually done by public-interest groups and published by them without a strong peer-review process. The most prominent is the Afterschool Alliance's annual opinion polls about after-school issues, which suggest that the general public is very supportive of after-school programs and concerned about the supervision, social development, and learning of children and adolescents when they are not in school. In a 2003 nationwide poll of registered voters, eight out of ten polled registered voters agreed with the statement that when thinking about children and after-school time, "afterschool programs are an absolute necessity for your community." In addition, 55 percent of registered voters surveyed believed there are not enough after-school programs in their area (Afterschool Alliance, 2003).[1] Duffett and Johnson found that "when it comes to having enough things for teenagers to do," a minority of parents surveyed say their community is doing as much as can be expected, compared to 65 percent of low income and 46 percent of higher-income parents who say it could realistically do much more (2004, 26). Seventy-one percent of minority parents agreed with the statement that the community could realistically do more.

Such findings need to be interpreted carefully. In particular, in the first survey respondents were asked to rate the importance of the issue without reference to other issues in a context of resource-allocation decisions. Those being polled were not asked to make any real

---

[1] http://www.afterschoolalliance.org/poll_jan_2004.pdf

trade-offs with other services or programs or to use their own money to fund programs. Under such circumstances, it is easy for respondents to express high levels of support for many types of programs or policies. In addition, while survey respondents indicated that more programs were needed in their area, this does not translate into specific numbers for expansion or to specific types of offerings needed.

Recent surveys have also attempted to identify specific types of offerings that might be needed. Duffett and Johnson found that 54 percent of their sample of parents agreed with the statement "Kids get more than enough academics during the school day, so after school programs should focus on other things that capture their interest" (2004, 31). However, 38 percent agreed with the statement "Since schools are putting so much emphasis on standardized tests and higher academic standards, kids are better off in after-school programs that focus on academic skills" (2004, 31). Low-income families and minorities were considerably more likely to want after-school programs that emphasized academic activities. In addition, they found that low-income parents were considerably less likely to report finding programs that are affordable, run by trustworthy adults, conveniently located, age-appropriate, interesting to their children, and of high quality. Parents also reported that finding appropriate summer programs was a significant challenge. Such an inventory of what parents want in a program, however, does not tell a policymaker whether a specific local program that offers these features will be used.

A study by Public Agenda (Farkas, Duffett, and Johnson, 2000), based on phone surveys and interviews of parents of children under five, parents of children in school, and adults without children, found varying support for public funding of programs. When asked who should take primary responsibility for making sure families have child care for their children, approximately 60 percent of the parents surveyed indicated it should be the parents themselves. Only 22 percent indicated it should be government, and only 24 percent indicated that taxpayers should help pay the costs. Finally, parents with children under 18 given options for improving child care chose the following as very helpful: a bigger tax break (63 percent), six months paid parental leave (57 percent), and extending the school day to provide after-school programs (53 percent). Thirty-six percent of parents with children under 18 thought spending tax money to create a universal child-care system would be very helpful. This study also found that respondents preferred public policy that made it easier and more affordable for one parent to stay at home (62 percent) over public policy that improved the cost and quality of child care (30 percent).

Perhaps most intriguing, Farkas, Duffett, and Johnson (2000) found differences in views among advocacy groups, parents, and employers about what public policy should be. Advocates were far more likely to agree with the statement that high-quality, center-based child care was as preferable as parental care (only 9 percent of parents strongly agreed with this statement, while 36 percent of advocates did). And 62 percent of advocates preferred the universal child-care option, compared to 40 percent (see above) of parents when offered options for improving child care.

The sometimes contrasting findings of the existing surveys can be a function of the specific questions asked, the time frame in which they were asked, or the particular groups of respondents. The conclusion to be drawn is that at this time the national surveys and polls available do not provide convincing evidence for moving forward with universal coverage or a larger government role per se, but do point to the need to carefully consider options and their support among different groups. National surveys do not offer insights into what is needed and provided in local markets.

Assumption-Based Estimates of Unmet Demand

The second type of evidence comes from studies undertaken in recent years to estimate demand and supply for after-school programs (Halpern, 1999; Children Now, 2001; Wechsler, 2001). These studies, not reported in peer-reviewed forums, provide estimates of supply that are based on tabulations of all the licensed or reported slots of known after-school care providers, sometimes in specific states. The estimates of demand or need in each of these studies rests on an untested premise that every youth in a geographic region who fits a specific profile "needs" and demands an after-school slot. For example:

- Wechsler (2001) assumed that two-thirds of the Massachusetts population between ages 6 and 17 in families where both parents work would want to participate in a program and, thus, after assessing supply, concluded that demand outstripped supply by a two-to-one margin.
- Children Now (2001) assumed that all children between the ages of 5 and 14 in two-parent families where both parents work or in single-parent families where the parent works needed and demanded an after-school program slot. Again, the study estimates that demand outstrips supply by a two-to-one margin.
- Using a similar approach, Halpern (1999) looked at three cities—Boston, Chicago, and Seattle—and estimated that in two-parent families where both parents work and in single-parent families where the parent works after school, only 35 percent of 6–12-year-olds could be accommodated with an after-school slot.

The assumption underlying these studies concerning the need for slots is not substantiated. As indicated in the previous chapter, many parents will find and actually prefer that their children are supervised by relatives, friends, or home-based day-care providers, or believe their children can function well without supervision. Thus, the above estimates are based on unfounded assumptions of demand. Furthermore, even if well founded, these studies give little information about the types of program content needed or demanded, being based solely on supervision criteria. They give little information upon which a local community could plan the expansion, if needed, of services.

Program-Level Enrollment Data

In contrast to the above estimates of pent-up demand, surveys of providers that look at enrollment relative to capacity imply that utilization of existing slots in existing programs is low. The earliest information, now quite dated given the expansion in programs of the last decade, comes from the 1991 National Survey of Before- and After-School Care Programs, which revealed that enrollment was at 59 percent of capacity. In fact, some after-school programs reported vacancy rates in excess of 75 percent. Only about one-third of programs were operating at 75 percent or more of capacity. In addition, 90 percent of the before-school enrollments and 83 percent of the after-school enrollments were for children in grades K–3. Note that these figures refer to enrollment in actual slots and provide no information about daily attendance rates of enrolled students. These enrollment rates did not vary among areas serving mostly low-income or middle-income families (Sepannen et al., 1993).

An alternative way to measure expressed demand is to consider real participation data for existing programs. In the last several years, there has been a trend for evaluations to report utilization rates, most recently from a small but growing literature on program evaluations of large after-school programs. In contrast to provider surveys, program evaluations generally do not tell us what enrollment is compared to capacity, but they do convey information about whether there is a waiting list for a program—an indicator that a program is oversubscribed and, thus, that demand might exceed supply.[2]

In the ESS evaluation (Grossman, 2002), programs reported concerns that they needed to restrict enrollment, although they did not report having a waiting list. In the 21st CCLC evaluation (DOEd, 2003), very few elementary-school programs and none of the middle-school programs nationwide had a waiting list (a prerequisite for entry into the elementary-school sample). We found no other studies documenting waiting lists for programs.

Program-Level Attendance Data

The limited evidence from enrollment and wait lists that programs have empty slots (i.e., supply exceeds demand) is complemented by reported low rates of participation once students register for a program. The 21st CCLC and ESS evaluations reported comparable attendance

---

[2] We note that the wait-list indicator is not a better representation of demand than some of those described above. Within a local area, waiting lists at different providers could be redundant with each other, or reflect where demand is located but not what type of program content is desired.

rates of approximately 42–58 days per year (depending on the grade level) for grades K–5 and 26–32 days per year for middle-school participants (Grossman et al., 2002; DOEd, 2003). The denominator for these rates included students who enrolled and attended the program once during the school year (ESS) or three times in the first month (21st CCLC). In other words, for neither of these studies does overall participation refer to all students who originally registered. There were some registered students who occupied a slot, but did not attend the minimum number of sessions to be included in the calculation of an attendance rate. If they had been included, the average attendance rates would have been lower in both cases. How much lower is impossible to assess, since the percentage of registered students who failed to meet this criterion were not reported in either study.

The After-School Corporation (TASC) evaluation, in contrast, did report attendance rates for students who remained enrolled that were much higher than in the above evaluations. The evaluation reported 3.9 days per week for elementary-school students and 2.9 days per week for middle-school students (Reisner et al., 2002). However, without defining what *remained enrolled* means in this context, it is difficult to interpret the results.

Recognizing the definition and measurement problems across studies, Lauver, Little, and Weiss reviewed the data from 48 program evaluations and found "one of the most important findings in recent program evaluations is the low youth utilization of OST programs. If participants vote with their feet, then most of these programs are not appealing enough to keep them coming back" (2004, p. 2).

Implications

Given the belief that demand outstrips supply, the current trend in the field is to push for capacity expansion, seeking to fund and provide more slots to meet the presumed excess demand. Yet we found little published evidence to support this trend. The studies of actual programs that document they are oversubscribed and the low levels of attendance among registered participants is inconsistent with polling data and assumption-based estimates indicating current unmet demand.

Furthermore, each of these pieces of information, individually and in sum, falls far short of the type of information needed to justify and plan for supply expansion to meet the needs of families. There is little evidence to indicate the nature of unmet demand, should it exist. Is it for school-age child-care programs, academic-enrichment programs, or youth-development activities? Is it by some families and not others, in some areas and not others? This simply has not been assessed carefully, leaving decision makers with little firm information upon which to make choices.

Rather than encouraging rapid expansion, some resources could be spent in assessing demand and supply in local markets to provide decision makers with needed information. In particular, survey information from families as well as providers could assess the level of demand for types of content or services by ability to pay and assess the level of public support for provision of specific services. The ability to meet the expressed need could be assessed through surveys of providers as well as assessments of the quality of provision by consumers or by application of instruments designed to assess the quality of services and classify content. Such research, if done in at least several major markets, could give a much better appreciation for the extent of the problem, if in fact there is one.

Such caution prior to efforts to expand is justified. Expansion of services without this information can lead to the provision of further unwanted and unneeded programs. Expansion of subsidies can lead to greater supply of poor-quality programming or unneeded subsidization. Some leaders, given the level of information available, have argued against unbridled expansion in the field because of the trade-offs that might exist between quantity and quality in OST slots (Wilson-Ahlstrom et al., 2002; Forum for Youth Investment, 2003). As the Forum for Youth Investment observes, "Quantity becomes the enemy of quality when a 'something is better then nothing' mentality creeps in" (2003, p. 2). If capacity is pushed beyond actual (rather than assumed) demand, quality might be unnecessarily diluted.

As the next two chapters demonstrate, the current focus on increasing the number of after-school and other OST program slots might be detracting from the equally important and necessary business of understanding and improving quality programming in order to improve its effectiveness. Improving effectiveness and quality of these programs (the focus of Chapters Four and Five) may each result in increased demand for OST programs or provide a need for programs and decision makers to better understand how they can generate more demand for targeted users (the focus of Chapter Six). With these pieces in place, the field could then turn to better understanding how to build the capacity of organizations, communities, and the system as a whole to provide sufficient effective (Chapter Seven), quality OST programming to meet the demand.

CHAPTER FOUR

Potential Effectiveness of OST Programs

OST advocates have made multiple claims about what these programs, especially after-school programs, can accomplish for youth participants. The breadth of outcomes claimed for OST programs that California's 2002 Proposition 49 would support included reduced crime, improved grades and test scores, reduced course repetition, reduced school dropouts, and reduced need for remedial education (Attorney General of the State of California, 2002). The appeal of these claims is apparent in the fact that this proposition, which adds approximately a half billion dollars annually to the existing state after-school programs, was easily passed during a time when the state of California faced budget challenges.

Along with the greater access to public resources comes the demand to be accountable for achieving measurable effectiveness consistent with the objectives of the funding streams. If after-school programs can meet these objectives, then access to these funding streams will be more supportable. Both program implementers and policymakers need to understand what effects after-school programs have convincingly demonstrated they can accomplish, how they accomplished them, what contributing conditions were important, and what, if anything, can be said about how these effects are best achieved. To make decisions about the best way to spend limited resources, both program implementers and policymakers also need to be able to compare the relative costs of OST program approaches.

This chapter reviews the literature that addresses issues of program effectiveness. We define the effect or impact of the program as the change in the outcome measure of the program that was due to participation in the program as opposed to other factors affecting participants. Policymakers, program designers, and providers should be interested in whether the program produces an effect over and above what would have occurred without the program—not whether the outcome measure itself changed. In other words, measuring a change in the outcomes for participants does not tell decision makers whether the program was responsible or not.

We also note that this chapter does not address what outcomes programs *should* aim to achieve. This value judgment is for decision makers, program designers, and communities to address. We concentrate on what effects, among the ambitious outcomes claimed, programs have been shown to achieve in published evaluations.

We first describe the general nature of the literature: what effects have been measured, and what others in the field conclude about OST effectiveness based on several past syntheses of the literature on program evaluations. We supplement this review of existing syntheses with results from the most rigorous research designs to indicate that the findings vary by type of outcomes observed and by grade or age of the participant group. Note that we are not assessing the frequency or discussing the magnitudes of these effects across studies. Our purpose is to highlight where there is evidence that effects have been found in at least one program evaluation, relying heavily on the most rigorous program-evaluation designs. To finish off the discussion, we note some of the crosscutting issues identified throughout the literature on program evaluation, including cost-effectiveness. We end with implications.

We will conclude that, at best, group-based OST programs have achieved some but not all of the impacts commonly claimed by after-school advocates, and no one program has been shown to produce more than a few positive outcomes. Based on the evidence to date, we should not expect the average program to produce strong positive outcomes.

Nature of the Existing Program-Evaluation Literature

Fashola (1998) called the state of program evaluation in the OST field rudimentary, and Roth et al. (1998) characterized the field as having a paucity of high-quality program evaluations. We note here the general limits of the evaluation literature and of the conclusions that can be drawn from it.

Measured Effects

The program sponsors and the evaluators determined what outcomes to study. As an example, there have been several empirically based evaluations of OST programs' effects on academic achievement, but only one evaluation examined child-care arrangements. Therefore, not all outcomes of interest have been evaluated. Effects measured fall into one of four categories:

- *Changed safety and health.* Most programs offer to provide at least minimal provision of child care through adult supervision in a safe setting.
- *Changed attitudes toward or actual changes in achievement (test scores) or levels of attainment (continuation to next grade, high school graduation, jobs).* Programs with these goals typically offer activities like tutoring, homework assistance, small learning groups, writing projects, field trips, college trips, discussions of job requirements and salaries, help with college applications that are designed to change motivation or provide the conditions for, and content needed, for academic success.
- *Changed social and health behaviors.* Programs can be specifically targeted toward these improved behaviors or hope to attain them through more generic activities. For example, some programs offer specific interventions aimed at preventing violence and drug use; others might assert impacts on these areas through drug counseling, positive youth-development activities, and general health education.
- *Changed social interactions.* By changing who youth spend time with, many programs assert that they can affect social interactions. Some specifically offer activities such as conflict-resolution training, anger management, peer discussion of important topics to youth, and parent support groups.

Finally, many OST programs also include a cultural-enrichment component through such activities as drama, visual arts and crafts projects, dance and movement instruction, and creative writing. However, cultural enrichment, beyond simple exposure itself, has rarely if ever been assessed as an outcome and does not appear in the studies we review.

OST programs might have impacts not just on youth but also on parents and caregivers, as well as on communities and society more generally (e.g., crime reduction). Impacts beyond those on youth have not been measured convincingly to date; therefore this analysis is confined to direct program affects on youth participants.

Internal Validity, or Whether the Evaluations Measured and Isolated Program Effects

The conclusions to be drawn from the program evaluations are only valid if the research design properly controlled for other factors impacting the participants and nonparticipants and isolated the effect due to the program. Most evaluations of OST programs use either observational or quasi-experimental study designs and control for important independent factors, such as family income, prior achievement, and so on that might effect the outcome, or dependent variable. With the exception of a few experimental studies included in our review, the fundamental problem with these study designs is they do not adequately control for selection bias (Fashola, 1998; Chaplin and Puma, 2003; Hollister, 2003).[1]

Selection bias refers to the fact that children who participate in voluntary activities differ from children who do not participate, and that such differences, as opposed to the programs themselves, might be associated with academic and nonacademic outcomes. In particular, those who self-select to join programs might have significantly different motivations or aspirations than those who choose not to participate, and this characteristic can affect the measured outcome. Thus, without proper controls one might conclude that the program caused

---

[1] Some studies using correlation models and quasi-experimental designs attempt to statistically control for these differences using measured characteristics (such as child's grade, sex, race, or ethnicity), but these do not adequately control for selection bias or motivation, as shown by Chaplin and Puma (2003) using the Prospect Study.

changes in outcomes, when in fact the motivation of participants in the treatment group was a major cause of outcome changes.

Selection bias can be controlled by use of random assignment to the treatment versus control group in an experimental design. This more rigorous design has been used in several studies. However, this research design is sometimes compromised by not properly controlling participation levels. As Hollister (2003, p. 9) points out, one study randomly assigned students applying to a program to the treatment or control group, thus ensuring that the two groups were similar in every way (including motivation to sign up). In the analysis, however, the treatment group only included students who attended the program at least 50 percent of the time and sometimes at least 80 percent of the time, while the control group included the students who did not receive the intervention and the students who had low attendance. While preferences and choice were initially controlled for at the time of assignment to treatment or control group, selection bias in terms of attendance seriously compromised the integrity of the study. More generally, most studies of program effects do not control for the level of participation after enrollment, thus introducing selection bias back into the design as students choose their own level of participation or treatment for unknown reasons. This reduces the researcher's ability to distinguish between program effects and effects associated with student characteristics that drive participation levels. The bottom line is that probably most of the studies in the field suffer from selection bias that potentially overstates the positive effect of the program on participants.

Generalizability and External Validity

Even if the evaluation was conducted to ensure internal validity and decision makers were confident that the results of the study accurately reflected the impact of the program on outcomes, the field further suffers from issues of whether and how the results of specific program evaluations can be generalized to other programs. The program-effects literature is a series of individual program evaluations undertaken for varying reasons at various times with various outcome measures. The evaluation results of existing programs cannot be inferred as applying to all programs, most programs, or the average program. As Blau and Currie conclude from their analysis of evaluation of programs, "it is a leap to argue that the average available after school program has any effect on child outcomes, since the model programs [those evaluated] appear to be significantly better than the typical program" (2003, p. 60).

Findings in the Literature

With these cautions in mind, we now turn to the published results of program evaluations. We first describe the results reported in existing syntheses: Fashola (1998), Scott-Little, Hamann, and Jurs (2002), Hollister (2003), Lauer et al. (2003), Miller (2003), and Kane (2004). These tend to be at a very general level. The results in individual studies, however, do vary by grade of participant and by outcome observed. In reporting these more detailed results we chose to rely only on published studies using experimental designs with random assignment that focused only on group-based OST programs and that underwent a peer-review process. The syntheses described either included less than rigorous evaluations in their reviews (Fashola, 1998; Lauer et al., 2003; Miller, 2003; Kane, 2004), examined non-group-based OST programs (Scott-Little, Hamann, and Jurs, 2002; Hollister, 2003), or a combination of the two (Fashola, 1998; Lauer et al., 2003; Miller, 2003). Detailed findings are reported only from the seven studies using experimental designs found in Table 4.1. The table is sorted by intended participant group.

Findings from Existing Syntheses

In trying to understand what effects OST programs have actually produced, we reviewed several well-known literature syntheses published over the last five years: Fashola (1998), Scott-Little, Hamann, and Jurs (2002), Hollister (2003), Lauer et al. (2003), Miller (2003), and Kane (2004). We summarize the content of each of these reviews in Appendix A, noting the types of studies included, limits identified, and general findings.

A review of the syntheses above allows the conclusion that specific OST programs might have had modest positive effects on several out-

Table 4.1
Peer-Reviewed Experimental Design Studies Evaluating Group-Based OST Programs

Program	Outcomes
Elementary-School Children	
Bicultural Competence (Schinke et al., 1988)	Substance-use behaviors
21st CCLC (DOEd, 2003, 2004)	School-age care arrangements, supervision in after-school hours, school attendance, homework completion, grades, feelings of safety, classroom effort, parent involvement in school events
Middle-School Children	
Carrera-Model Teen Program (Philliber et al., 2002)	Sexual activity, contraceptive use, pregnancy, access to good health care
Creating Lasting Connections (Johnson et al., 1996)	Communication with peers and family, bonding with parents
Friendly PEERsuasions (Weiss and Nicholson, 1998)	Substance use
High-School Children	
Carrera-Model Teen Program (Philliber et al., 2002)	Sexual activity, contraceptive use, pregnancy, access to good health care
Upward Bound (Myers and Schirm, 1999)	College attendance, student educational expectations

comes of interest, including achievement tests, grades, attainment, reduced substance abuse, relationships with peers and parents, completion of high school, and reduced teen-pregnancy rate. These positive outcomes varied by program, and in most cases, while statistically significant, were small. These same reviews, however, raised significant questions regarding the biases and methodological flaws in the existing evaluation base, such that one should hesitate to draw strong inferences.

Evidence Concerning School-Age Care

At a minimum, one expects that school-age OST programs provide a safe and supervised setting. Many argue that after-school care programs improve the safety of the community and the participants, presumably because the participants are being supervised. Another potential benefit of increasing supervised care of children is that parents and guardians might feel more comfortable working, and therefore more inclined to work, knowing that their youth will be safe. This impact has not been assessed.

The only program evaluation in Table 4.1 that examined impacts on school-age care arrangements and related outcomes was the 21st CCLC evaluation. Less rigorous evaluations of other major after-school programs also fail to measure this (Kane, 2004). Surprisingly, both first- and second-year results of the 21st CCLC evaluation did not find that the program increased the number of children who were in a supervised setting during after-school hours. The evaluation found that students in these programs would have been in an alternative supervised setting cared for by a parent or a sibling; therefore, total numbers of children in supervised settings did not increase as a result of offering the program. The results showed that the elementary-grade-level participants did not report feeling any safer than those who did not attend in the first year, but second-year results showed a change, with treatment students report- ing feeling safer, by a slight margin, than those who did not attend. It is not clear if parents and siblings were using the availability of centers to free up their own time or if they believed that the centers would provide a better and safer place to be than they could offer.

Evidence Concerning Academic Achievement and Attainment

Two of the programs listed in Table 4.1 were evaluated with respect to academics, including behavior in school, such as school attendance, parental involvement, educational expectation, grades and test scores, and attainment. Positive effects were found for each.

Behavior in school. Compared to students not in programs, the 21st CLCC elementary-school participants in both the first and second year were no more likely to report higher rates of homework comple- tion or teacher's satisfaction with completed assignments, nor did such participants have significantly higher rates of school attendance or have greater teacher reports about effort spent on schoolwork. This seems surprising given that homework help is a key component for many OST programs, especially after-school care programs. Moreover, the 21st CCLC had a high proportion of teacher staff (three out of five program staff members are regular school-day teachers), which was qualified to ensure that homework was completed satisfactorily.

Parental involvement. Only the 21st CCLC evaluation examined differences in parental involvement for program participants compared to nonparticipants. A higher degree of parental involvement by participant's families compared to comparison families was consistently found in the 21st CCLC evaluation for the elementary-school sample in both years. For example, parents of elementary-school participants were more likely to report that they helped their child with homework at least three times last week. It is not clear if, how, or why parents of participants became more involved during the course of the year in this program. Parents with a child in the program were also significantly less likely to agree that their child works hard at school (although there was no significant effect on teacher reports about school effort).

Educational expectations. The experimental evaluation of Upward Bound, a precollege program for students who traditionally are less likely to attend college (i.e., from low-income families or children of recent immigrants), found a significant increase in the students' (but not their parents') educational expectations. Other research demonstrates that educational expectations are very strongly related to eventual educational attainment (House 1992a, 1992b). No other program evaluations using an experimental design measured impacts on expectations.

Grades and standardized test scores. In general, the OST programs reviewed did not show evidence of an impact on test scores. Participants in the elementary 21st CCLCs did not have significantly higher grades or better test scores than nonparticipants.

High-school credits, graduation, and postsecondary education. Unlike grades and standardized test scores, at least one OST program had a clear, positive impact on the number of credits earned and on graduation rates. Youth who were randomly assigned to the Upward Bound program earned significantly more high-school credits and were significantly more likely to graduate than youth who were assigned to the control group.

Evidence Concerning Social Behavior

A number of programs whose primary objective included avoidance of risky behavior showed positive effects using the most rigorous evaluation methods (i.e., experimental design). One example is the Children's Aid Society Carrera-Model Teen Pregnancy Prevention Program, a year-round after-school program for middle- and high-school students designed to reduce pregnancy, which increased knowledge about safe sexual behavior, reduced teen pregnancy, and promoted youth development. Participants randomly assigned to the program had significantly lower odds of being sexually active, of failure to use a condom or hormonal contraceptive method if sexually active, or of having a pregnancy. They were more likely to report receipt of good-quality primary health care and were more knowledgeable about the potential effects of being sexually active three years after entering the program. Other programs that showed significant positive impacts in reducing risky behaviors were the Bicultural Competence and Friendly PEERsuasion.

Only one evaluation of a program whose primary objective was not risk reduction collected information on risky behaviors—the 21st CCLC evaluation. In that evaluation, there were no impacts on risky behaviors for elementary-school students randomly assigned to a 21st CCLC.

Evidence Concerning Social Interactions

Social interactions, such as improving interpersonal skills and bonding with significant others, were less studied than behavioral or academic outcomes. The evaluations of the 21st CCLC and Creating Lasting Connections, a church-based program seeking to reduce substance use among high-risk youth, tested but failed to find significant impacts on interpersonal skills, or increases in the incidence of "leveling" about substance use, "leveling" with close friends, "leveling" about school-work, and bonding with mother or bonding with father.

Evidence by Grade Level

Program effects, and programs themselves, appear to vary by grade level, although there is not enough evidence to be conclusive.

Elementary-grade students. The only unambiguous positive academic impact for elementary-grade children was increased parental involvement (in the 21st CCLC evaluation), which many argue is correlated with academic outcomes. No evaluations with random-assignment designs demonstrated positive impacts for academic achievement outcomes, such as standardized tests and grades. There is rigorous evidence from the Bicultural Competence Evaluation (Schinke et al., 1988) that OST programs can reduce the onset of risky behaviors for children in elementary grades.

A main concern for parents of young children is ensuring that their children have a safe, supervised setting when they are not at home. While generally the literature reviewed ignored this essential outcome, the one exception (21st CCLC) failed to find any increase in the number of children in supervised settings during OST.

Evidence of impact on outcomes for middle-school students. The Carrera-Model Teen Program showed that a program that specifically targeted high-risk behaviors did successfully reduce these behaviors in this age group.

Evidence of impact on high-school students. The two programs that focused on high-school students showed positive impact. We note that both programs had been carefully designed in terms of program content to achieve such effects. Compared to their peers, high-school participants in the Upward Bound precollege programs reported higher educational expectations, earned higher grades, earned more credits, were more likely to graduate, and were more likely to attend a postsecondary education institution or receive training after graduation. Participants in the Carrera-Model Teen Program that targeted risky behaviors, such as sexual activity and substance abuse, likewise showed positive impacts. Participants were less likely to become sexually active, fail to use a condom or contraceptive method if sexually active, or have a pregnancy.

Other Findings and Issues Raised

In this section, we discuss other important issues raised by this review. They include the impact of participation on outcomes, reasonableness of expectations for some types of outcomes, the need to pay attention to program content and implementation to ensure positive results, assessing whether the program works on specific populations, and cost-effectiveness.

Participation Effects

A significant assumption behind many programs is that, up to some point, greater intensity and duration of attendance and participation in the program is beneficial. Little and Harris (2003), of the Harvard Family Research Project, undertook an extensive review of program evaluations that show a relationship between participation and outcomes. Most, but not all, evaluations showed the expected positive relationship between duration and positive outcomes or intensity and positive outcomes.

While indications are positive, these studies do not allow one to conclude that greater participation causes greater benefits. Participants could choose how often or intensely they participated in a program. Because these evaluations reviewed were almost all quasi-experimental, it is at least as likely that the observed relationship between participation and positive outcomes reflects the fact that students with better outcomes are more likely to persist in a program or activity than students without positive outcomes. Alternatively, those with preexisting high levels of motivation to participate might exhibit greater participation levels than those without high motivation. This could artificially inflate measures of impact unless motivation is controlled for.

To convincingly assess the impact of duration or intensity on outcomes, one needs an evaluation design that essentially removes selection bias from the relationship between participation and outcomes. This might mean, for example, randomly assigning students to participate in programs that vary in duration or intensity or using some other method whereby the decision to participate at higher versus lower levels is not made by the youth or based on characteristics related to the youth prior to beginning the program. In addition, one would need to carefully collect attendance records tracking both control- and treatment-group participation patterns—a costly and difficult undertaking.

Few studies will be able to convincingly test whether participation is linked to outcomes or determine what the minimum level of participation required is to meet program goals. Nevertheless, it is important to track participation in a consistent manner so that comparisons can be made over time and across program and regions. The studies that do track participation often define it very broadly—whether or not a youth participated at all as opposed to the level of participation (Chaput, Simpkins, Little, and Weiss, 2004).[2]

There is a growing awareness of the need for proper monitoring in the field, and efforts are being made to address the need (see, e.g., Fiester, 2004). But answering the question of how much participation is adequate to produce the desired outcomes is proving difficult. At this point, statistical analysis of survey data, or statistical modeling of the participation effect in experimental designs that do not control for participation, might be the best that can be practically accomplished.

Establishing Reasonable Expectations for Academic Achievement

Kane (2004) argues that the education field usually judges a classroom intervention to have been effective if it shows a positive impact of 0.10 to 0.30 standard deviations in test scores, about what is produced with six months of regular schooling. To show such effects usually requires a large sample to support the statistical tests needed to draw significant conclusions. Kane then observes that the average hours of academic instruction in an after-school program should lead one to expect much weaker impact, on the order of 0.02 to 0.05 standard deviations. The low end assumes an average low level of attendance, and the high end assumes perfect daily attendance. Few OST programs have the number of attendees needed for the sample sizes required to measure impacts of this low a magnitude. He concludes that the field should not expect to see strong impacts by OST programs due to both the level of intervention being relatively weak and the inability to measure such weak effects given sample size constraints.

Because of this, Granger and Kane (2004) argue for more modest expectations regarding test-score results and a greater focus on more easily detected intermediate impacts, such as parental involvement in school-related activities,[3] homework completion, school attendance, and grades.

---

[2] Chaput (2004) notes that evaluation studies should include measures for participation that account for intensity (the amount of time a youth participated in an activity in a given period), duration (the number of years or period that a youth participated), and breadth (the variety of participation across programs).

[3] Though we urge caution in interpreting greater parental involvement as reflecting positively on a program's impact, for reasons discussed earlier in this chapter.

Paying Attention to Program Content and Implementation to Ensure Positive Impact

Several different authors argue for more attention to program content and implementation to ensure positive impacts.

Fashola (1998) and Roth and Brooks-Gunn (2003) both noted that a close alignment between program content and assessed outcomes might produce stronger evaluation results. For example, as we described, the results were disappointing for the 21st CCLC programs (which involved an experimental design for the elementary-school centers), where content was not closely linked to the outcomes measured, nor was it controlled across sites. In contrast, two programs that were successful in impacting academic and behavioral outcomes were structured to do so. Upward Bound, the college-preparation program, and the Carrera Program, whose objective was to reduce pregnancy rates and "empower youth," both had content and components strongly linked to these outcomes.

In a similar vein, evaluators argue that evaluations need to more carefully track and describe the intervention itself to both generalize the program findings as well as to attempt to use the findings to produce similar results. For example, the Joblessness and Urban Poverty Research Program noted that "policymakers and program developers must be cautious when concluding that a program is ineffective based on outcome evaluations that do not include an implementation analysis" (2001, p. 6). Hollister (2003) points to a specific example of this problem. The evaluation of QOP indicated positive impact of the program over several sites. But a closer review of the findings indicated that "one site failed completely and was not included in the analysis. All the significant academic outcomes were isolated in the Philadelphia site. . . . Lower childbearing did not occur at the Philadelphia site and only came from the pooling across sites, several of which suffered from attrition bias" (Hollister, 2003, p. 10). In short, better information on the intervention is needed to ensure that the participants really did receive an intervention that was different than nonparticipants, and to understand what program descriptors would be important to reproduce if similar results are desired.

While we saw some positive outcomes in the program evaluations, several studies indicate the possibility of negative outcomes. Although inconclusive because of the quasi-experimental study design, middle-school students in 21st CCLC after-school programs had worse outcomes than nonparticipants. Middle-school program participants were more likely to report selling illegal drugs and having had property damaged than nonparticipants. In other words, it may not be a given that the average after-school program can assume it readily avoids doing harm (a central tenet of any intervention). This might especially be the case for programs targeting early adolescents, where aggregation of students with problem behaviors has been shown in other settings to reinforce, rather than reduce, problem behaviors. Dishion and his colleagues (1991, 1999) suggest that this type of grouping that produces negative results can be a special problem during early adolescence (e.g., middle school).

Taken together, these three arguments offer reasons to pay particular attention to program content and implementation to improve the understanding of program effects and to improve that ability to achieve them in other sites.

Program Targeting

Many larger evaluations disaggregate a sample according to major demographic, educational, or other characteristics to assess whether impacts are stronger for some subgroups. If impacts are found for some subgroups only, a program can be more cost-effective by targeting those subgroups that benefit most. Alternatively, program designers can attempt to develop components that better meet the needs of the groups not being served.

Some of the analyses examined differential impact by racial or ethnic group. For example, Upward Bound, the college-preparation program that provided long-term, intensive services for youth who were believed to be unlikely to graduate from high school or seek postsecondary education, yielded small but significant impacts when viewed across all participants. When the sample was disaggregated according to level of the student's educational expectation when he or she first entered the program, however, many of the benefits accrued to the small percentage of interested students who had the lowest expectations at the beginning of the program. If the program had effectively targeted only these students, then it is likely to have shown stronger impacts per participant. Alternatively, with this information, it could begin to develop program components that could more effectively serve the larger group of participants.

Needed Cost Information

While a specific program or type of program might be determined to have a sizable positive impact, it is possible that the benefits of pursuing such programs are mitigated by the costs of operating the programs. Thus, policymakers and program implementers are increasingly interested in knowing about the cost of programs relative to their benefits. Such information is particularly useful in time of budget crises, and policymakers that do not have a vested interest in specific programs want to know the relative costs and benefits of different options when it comes time to allocate resources, be they public or private, among an array of programs or program components. Program implementers want to know whether a candidate intervention has demonstrable benefits that match or exceed the costs of a program. Being able to make sound resource-allocation decisions would be attractive to various stakeholders, such as funders, families, and the implementing organization.

At this point in time, however, little consistent information has been gathered that would allow such analysis. In some cases, the cost information is based on questionable assumptions or guesses rather than careful collection and analysis of information from operating programs.

Wechsler (2001) convened a working group to make estimates of what it would cost to provide high-quality OST programming in Massachusetts, incorporating salaries and wages, transportation, insurance, rent, and basic administrative costs. The author concluded that an OST program that covered the time after school during the school year would cost $4,349 per child (25 hours per week for 38 weeks).

Newman, Smith, and Murphy (1999) collected cost information from preventive and youth-development programs (Table 4.2) to calculate the cost of programming per hour per youth. Averaging across the distribution of youth and time participating, the authors calculate that the average cost of OST programming is $2.55 per hour per

Table 4.2
Calculating the Cost of Preventive and Youth Development Programs

Organization	Annual Cost/Youth	Hours/Youth
Teen Outreach Program	$572	260
The After-School Corporation	$1,000	540
Boys & Girls Club	$139	n/a
Girl Scouts of America	$135	n/a

SOURCE: Newman, Smith, and Murphy, 2000.

youth, for a total of $3,060 for 1,200 hours annually. It is not clear from these estimates what percentage of the annual cost per youth is fixed versus variable. Nor is it possible to determine the cost of serving an additional youth, nor how much it would cost other organizations to replicate these programs.

Grossman et al. (2002) collected actual cost profiles for ten after-school sites participating in the ESS Initiative. These provided what appear to be the most thorough calculation of total cash and noncash expenditures, including administrative salaries, snacks, transportation, custodians, youth activities, and other administrative costs. The average cost per program was $149,620 annually for 33 weeks of programming, operating 4.7 days per week. Programs served an average of 63 youths, for a total cost of $15 per day per youth.

More efforts need to be made to determine the fixed, variable, and marginal costs of programs. While Grossman et al. (2002) have made a valiant first attempt toward more reliable approaches, more work along these lines must be done to define terms, standardize approaches, collect detailed information using those standard definitions and approaches, and tie these cost estimates to program impact in a meaningful manner accounting minimally for the location, content, purpose, and institutional setting of the program. Once cost information is available, it can be combined with program impacts to better understand the cost-effectiveness of different options. Perhaps in later years or for specific programs, impacts can be tracked over the long term to understand the full cost-benefit of OST programming.

Implications

Advocates are making different claims about the effectiveness of OST programs. To assess the likelihood that subsidized group-based programs could be expected to meet these claims, we reviewed the OST program-evaluation literature.

Our review of the literature found very few well-designed studies from which firm conclusions could be drawn. Even well-designed studies failed to account for the effect of participants' motivation on program participation, participation level, or content and implementation variation. Furthermore, the literature does not allow one to make conclusions about the field as a whole, but only specific programs. Thus these findings represent what might be possible, not what is.

Analysis of the program evaluations targeted to the OST programs this report focuses on and that used rigorous experimental designs suggests that, at best, some programs have produced modest positive effects in the following areas: academic outcomes (parental involvement, educational expectations, credits attained and graduation rates) and social behavioral outcomes (sexual activity and pregnancy). No program we found influenced all of these outcomes; indeed, all of these outcomes were not assessed for a single program. Furthermore, program impact varied by grade levels.

We conclude that claims about the broad benefits of OST programming are overstated. We do not know with any certainty that much of what is being claimed is positively proven. Most programs would not have all the effects mentioned or even some of these effects. Possible positive impacts cannot be assumed for the average program, most not having been carefully constructed to produce the specific impacts studied.

Policymakers and program funders can help improve the current state of knowledge with concerted and targeted efforts. First, they can support panels or other discussion mechanisms to review evidence and articulate more clearly what expectations for impacts are reasonable given what is currently known, a point made by Granger and Kane (2004). More work should be done to set realistic expectations for outcome impact, given the limited participation, varying content, and varying implementation across sites in average programs.

Second, policymakers can ensure that funding for further evaluations go to studies with strong controls for selection bias; accurate measurement of and accounting for participation and, when possible, careful assessment of the relationship between participation and outcomes; documentation of the content and implementation across sites and across time to improve the ability to replicate programs that are proven effective; and tracking of effects for age groups or other important subgroups to enable targeting when appropriate. These evaluations should match the evaluation outcomes to the stated goals of the program.

Third, policymakers can promote the use of funds to collect adequate cost information on programs that are deemed worthy of a rigorous evaluation. Finally, because so little is understood about the cost-effectiveness of group-based OST when compared to other options to meet the same objectives, policymakers should remain cautious about investing in these programs without better information on alternatives.

We note that this discussion is not intended to imply that all programs should be so rigorously evaluated, given the costs involved. A two-pronged approach could be used. Large, publicly funded programs that reach many participants should be subject to rigorous evaluation against the stated objectives of the funding stream. For other programs, initial, less expensive analyses can help select programs for evaluation that are designed and supported in ways likely to have and be able to show impacts (Walker, 2004). Thus, we argue for careful selection of programs for evaluation to cost-effectively increase information of program impact.

CHAPTER FIVE

Assessment of Quality in OST Programs

In Chapter Four, we reviewed the most rigorously evaluated group-based OST programs to assess what OST programs can potentially expect to accomplish. With the exception of the 21st CCLC programs, most of the programs that were rigorously evaluated could be considered model programs (e.g., the Carrera-Model Teen Program). Providers who hope to improve their programs have two options. They can replicate a model program that has been proven to be effective at attaining desired outcomes, or they can work to ensure that the program components, management, and environment comply with what is known or believed to constitute "quality" in the context of an OST setting. Because many OST programs are homegrown and generally emphasize the idiosyncratic philosophy and experiences of their founders, the concept of adopting program components shown to be associated with positive outcomes is very attractive and has received considerable attention in the OST field. To do the latter requires evidence of which program characteristics have been shown to produce the desired impacts.

In this chapter we focus on relevant literature that attempts to identify those specific aspects of programs that are believed to be associated with positive outcomes. We examined three distinct literatures that fall under the OST umbrella or are distinctly related: school-age-care, youth-development, and education literature. Compared to the previous chapter, the strength of the evidence reviewed in this chapter is weaker. None of the studies use an experimental design to assess program-factor impact on outcomes, and only a few used a quasi-experimental design. We found a handful of studies that used correlation models, and many studies that used expert opinion to determine what program features influence the quality of a program. Thus the review of program factors contains less rigorous evidence upon which to base policy.

We first discuss the literature sources. We then discuss the three literatures we judged to provide some useful insights in possible important program factors. After this we summarize across these three literatures to show the common program elements held to be important in producing desired outcomes. Finally, we draw out policy implications.

We find that there is a convergence among these different studies on a set of factors believed to be associated with the outcomes measures used. We conclude with a strong caveat that the field should consider these factors as the field's best guess about program qualities that might lead to positive outcomes. These factors can provide general guidance to those seeking to design new programs or improve existing programs without adopting a model program. They offer hypotheses that can be tested in more rigorous designs.

Literature Sources

As shown in Table 5.1, we turned to the school-age-care, youth-development, and education literatures to assess what can be learned about quality in OST programs. We include several education studies because they consider many of the same characteristics of schools and classrooms that are thought to be important in an OST setting. In some cases, there has been much more rigorous assessment of the impact of these characteristics in the education literature, thus strengthening the evidence base for these findings.

The school-age-care literature is the weakest of these three sets of literatures, and the youth-development and education literature are more or less equally rigorous (though still less rigorous than program evaluations used in Chapter Four to assess potential program impacts).

In addition, we draw on other related sources from education, such as the effective-school literature, class-size studies, and recent studies on teacher-training effects.

Table 5.1
Literatures and Sources Used to Identify Program Factors Associated with Positive Youth Outcomes

Literature	Source
School-age care	Beckett, Hawken, and Jacknowitz, 2001 NSACA, 1998 Pierce, Hamm, and Vandell, 1999 Rosenthal and Vandell, 1996
Youth development	Gambone, Klem, and Connell, 2002 NRC and IOM, 2002 Roth and Brooks-Gunn, 2003 Vandell et al., 2004
Education	*Effective schools* (Purkey and Smith, 1983; National Research Council, 1997; Haycock, 2001) *Class Size* (Glass and Smith, 1979; Glass et al., 1982; Brewer et al., 1999; Krueger 1999; Molnar, 1999; Bohrnstedt and Stecher, 2002; AERA, 2003) *Teacher Training* (Angrist and Lavy, 1998; Jacob and Lefgren, 2002)

We recognize that the education research is related to, but is not part of, OST programming. Transferring program factors found in related fields to the OST field might not be straightforward. Moreover, it is likely that the relative importance of factors to one field is not the same as in a related field. For example, the lessons learned from the education field are most likely to pertain to OST programs that are intended to support educational outcomes, and would not necessarily be applicable to ones focusing on more general youth outcomes.

The School-Age-Care Literature

The school-age-care field—which generally focuses on children in elementary grades and less often middle-school grades—is most concerned with programs whose emphasis is on providing school-age care or a safe, supervised place for students who do not otherwise have adult supervision.

Findings from Statistical Correlations

The most influential research in the school-age-care area is by Deborah Vandell and her colleagues (e.g., Kim Pierce and Jill Hamm). Their research establishes that in different samples of children from low-income families there is a strong and significant statistical correlation between positive outcomes, such as better adjustment in school and positive staff-child interactions, and factors like total enrollment, staff-child ratios, and staff education.

Pierce, Hamm, and Vandell (1999) studied the adjustment of 150 first-graders in 37 after-school programs by observing the children in the day-care setting and classroom. They found two day-care-setting practices that were correlated with better adjustment in school: program flexibility and staff interactions. For boys, staff positivity, as expressed toward the children, was associated with boys manifesting few adjustment problems in school and externalizing behaviors. Staff negativity was associated with boys receiving lower grades. Program flexibility was associated with boys displaying better social skills.

In another study, the number of negative staff-child interactions observed in a program was positively correlated with children's perceptions of overall climate and emotional support (Rosenthal and Vandell, 1996). In other words, observer-rated emotional climate was positively related to students' assessments, at least for this age group. Further, researcher-observed positive or neutral staff-child interactions were positively correlated with the autonomy and privacy that children experience in a program.

Rosenthal and Vandell (1996) investigated the relationship between program features and program quality. A higher number of observed negative staff-child interactions were associated with larger staff-to-child ratios, lower staff education, and fewer program activities. In programs where directors reported a large number of different activities offered in a week, researchers more frequently observed positive or neutral staff-child interactions; moreover, children's perceptions of the overall climate of the program and emotional support received from the staff were higher. Children reported poorer emotional climate in programs with larger total enrollment and those with a higher number of observed negative child-staff interactions.

In general, these programs factors are useful because program providers can easily operationalize them.

Findings Based on Expert Opinion

Beyond the relatively small body of statistical-correlation studies produced by Vandell and her associates, the literature depends heavily on convergence of expert opinion.

Several expert panels emphasize the importance of having a positive emotional climate, including fostering a warm relationship between staff and students and between staff and parents as well as having positive staff-staff relations; encouraging and respecting students; making children feel welcome, relaxed, and safe (NSACA, 1998; National Association of Elementary School Principals [NAESP], 1999; NRC and IOM, 2000); and fostering mutual respect among staff and volunteers (NIOST, 2000).[1] Programs are advised that they can establish a positive emotional climate by hiring staff that are warm and caring toward children and that take the time to establish a relationship or by providing training to staff in these areas (Miller and Marx, 1990; NSACA, 1998; NAESP, 1999; Newman, Smith, and Murphy, 1999).

Several experts argue that offering an array of activities yields several benefits, including fostering decision-making skills and creativity; providing time and space for physical play (such as running, jumping, and climbing); providing time for the emotional releases that come from art, dramatic play, and sand and water play; and capturing participants' interests (which is important for increasing retention rates, particularly at older ages) (Alexander, 1986; Belle, 1997).

RAND Synthesis

In 2001, RAND published a synthesis of the after-school-care literature within the elementary-age child-care tradition to identify the key structural and process factors shown or upheld by experts in the field to be associated with high-quality after-school programs or positive child outcomes (educational attainment, emotional development, health, etc.).

---

[1] Volunteers are believed to improve the range of activities and instruction that can be provided to participants beyond what paid staff can offer and reduce the student-staff ratio.

The studies reviewed were at varying levels of reliability below the gold standard of experimental research and included several of the studies mentioned above. The RAND researchers weighted each study on the basis of the relative confidence in the recommended practices[2] and calculated a weighted average across studies for support for particular program factors. On this basis, the program factors were judged to have strong, moderate, or limited support in the literature.

Table 5.2 below summarizes the 15 quality indicators identified in the research synthesis across three categories, with boldface entries indicating that the practice had strong, as opposed to moderate or limited, support in the literature.

The Youth-Development Literature

Over the past decade, the youth-development field has increasingly moved from prevention programs to keep youth problem-free to think-

Table 5.2
Indicators of a Quality After-School Care Program Identified in RAND Synthesis

Staff Characteristics	Program Characteristics	Community Contacts
Training	Variety of activities	Family involvement
Education	Flexible programming	Use of volunteers
Compensation	Emotional climate	Community partnerships
	Child-to-staff ratio	
	Total enrollment	
	Mixing of age groups	
	Age-appropriate activities	
	Space availability	
	Continuity and complementarity with day-school programs	
	Clear goals and evaluation of program	
	Materials	
	Attention to safety and health	

SOURCE: Beckett, Hawken, and Jacknowitz, 2001.

---

[2] For example, the researchers placed the most confidence in conclusions based on positive correlations between quality indicators and desirable outcome and the least confidence in recommendations or conclusions based on anecdotal experience of a single practitioner.

ing about ways to proactively encourage youth to reach their full potential to develop the skills, knowledge, and other personal and social assets necessary to function well as an adolescent and eventually as an adult—for example, enter the workforce, be able to support a family, and function as a citizen (Gambone, Klem, and Connell, 2002). Reaching full potential includes a broad range of positive outcomes, such as developing "a sense of security and personal identity, and learn[ing] rules of behavior, expectations, values, morals and skills needed to move into healthy and productive adulthood" (NRC and IOM, 2002, p. 3). This emphasis on proactive support for reaching full potential has been accompanied by an emphasis on the role of community-based organizations, such as those that provide OST programming, to help because some believe that family, neighbors, and schools do not provide the supports many youth need.

Against this backdrop, the NRC and IOM jointly commissioned a panel to identify what program factors were associated with successful community programs.[3] The panel reviewed the theoretical literature on youth development, as well as the correlation studies that examine what features of the environment are consistent with or related to positive developmental outcomes, such as emotional well-being, school behaviors, and social interactions with parents and friends.

They argued that organizations that work with adolescents should strive to ensure that the environment within the organization provides adolescent participants with as many of these desirable features as possible. Table 5.3 lists and briefly describes these features.

To give a sense of the research underlying the features represented in the table, we describe the evidence used to derive two of the features: supportive relationships and opportunities to belong.

Supportive relationships. Theorists and researchers conclude that having supportive relationships with an adult—qualities of emotional support (e.g., caring and responsiveness) and instrumental support (e.g., providing useful guidance)—are important for positive youth development. Psychologists have noted that objective measures of emo-

---

[3] Roth and Brooks-Gunn (2003); Gambone, Klem, and Connell (2002); and Vandell et al. (2004) also developed lists of such factors from literature reviews. We rely heavily here on the NRC and IOM work, as it is now being used as a reference for the field as a whole. Lists by others are consistent with that in Table 5.2.

Table 5.3
Features of Positive Developmental Settings

Feature	Descriptor
Physical and psychological safety	Safe and health-promoting facilities
Appropriate structure	Limit setting; clear and consistent rules and expectations
Supportive relationships	Warmth; closeness; connectedness, communication
Opportunities to belong	Opportunities for meaningful inclusion
Positive social norms	Rules of behavior; ways of doing things
Support for efficacy and mattering	Empowerment practices that support autonomy
Opportunities for skill building	Opportunities to learn physical, intellectual, psychological, emotional, and social skills
Integration of family, school, and community efforts	Coordination; synergy among family, school, and community

SOURCE: NRC and IOM, 2002, Table 4.1.

tional or instrumental support are less important than the adolescent's perception of it (NRC and IOM, 2002).[4]

One line of correlation research that associates supportive relationships to positive youth outcomes relates characteristics of parents to positive youth development. Over time, positive parental support is associated with positive school motivation, mental health, and lower rates of risky behaviors (like drinking and smoking), delinquency, and school misconduct (Clark, 1983; Eccles, Lord, and Midgley, 1991; Epstein and Dauber, 1991; Henderson and Berla, 1994; Booth and Dunn, 1996, Grotevant, 1998; Furstenberg et al., 1999; Steinberg, 2001). A second research strand shows that supportive relationships are positively associated with desirable outcomes in other settings, including the classroom, sports programs, and Big Brothers and Big Sisters, and mentoring programs (Comer, 1988; Roberts and Treasure, 1992; Smoll, Smith, Barnett, and Everett, 1993; Seefeldt, Ewing, and Walk, 1993; Eccles, 1998; Grossman and Rhodes, 1999; Jackson and Davis, 2000).

Opportunities to belong. Correlational research establishes an association between feeling connected with schools and lower levels of

---

[4] In the school-age literature below, some evidence is cited to suggest that a child's perceptions of emotional support are correlated with objective measures of a positive emotional climate.

emotional stress, violent behavior, substance abuse, and delayed sexual initiation (Blum and Rhinehart, 1997). Students who say that they feel alienated and rejected by their teachers or schools are more likely to drop out (Fine, 1991; Roderick, 1991).

Limitations. Because it is difficult (and in most settings unethical) to manipulate adolescents' environments to substantially reduce or increase the features listed in Table 5.2, it is impossible to know whether modifying these features generally would improve developmental outcomes. This leads to the same selection bias that precludes a clear understanding of the causal relationships discussed in Chapter Four. Just as one could argue that these characteristics produce better developmental outcomes, one could argue that adolescents who are fortunate to be on the positive development path seek out environments with these features, or that because such adolescents are easier to deal with, their parents feel more able to be supportive.

These results, however, do offer hypotheses for OST programs that can be answered empirically: are these features, when manipulated, associated with changed developmental outcomes in OST programs, for whom, and in what combinations?

The Education Literature

In the education field, researchers have examined what types of learning or school environments are related to learning outcomes. Thus, the conclusions about what seems to work in school settings are likely to be most applicable to OST programs that emphasize learning outcomes. However, as we mentioned earlier, these findings would need to be applied carefully. This work is based on a combination of experimental designs, quasi-experimental designs, and other, less quantitative methods. The literature seeks to identify characteristics of effective schools, class-size effects, and teacher training that produce better educational results. These literatures are very large. Because the conclusions that are drawn are consistent with the school-age-care and youth-development findings, we keep this discussion very brief.

Effective Schools

The effective-schools literature seeks to identify characteristics of schools (and classrooms) that positively influence student outcomes (Purkey and Smith, 1983; NRC, 1997; Haycock, 2001). The primary characteristics of effective schools include

- a clear and focused mission
- strong leadership
- high expectations for student achievement
- strong instructional leadership and materials
- opportunity to learn and time on task
- a safe, orderly school environment
- frequent assessment of academic progress
- constructive home and school relations.

Because it is largely based on statistical correlation, the literature has several serious limitations. First, it is not clear what would happen if ineffective schools attempted to adopt effective-schools characteristics. No one has seriously tested whether application of these concepts is feasible in low-performing schools. Second, the strongest methodological design in this literature was quasi-experimental. The literature focuses at the school level, and it is not possible to draw inferences on the effects attributable to specific program components or their interactions.

Class Size

The Student/Teacher Achievement Ratio (STAR) study is one the best-known education studies that used random assignment to examine the impact of class-size reduction on student outcomes. Elementary-school students and teachers were randomly assigned to one of three types of classes, where most remained for three years: small classes, regular-size classes, and regular-size classes with a teacher's aide (Krueger, 1999). On average, students in small classes showed the greatest gains in standardized-test scores through the third grade. The evidence indicated that a maximum of 17 children produced stronger results. Studies failed to show desirable effects when there were 20 versus 25 children in the classroom (American Educational Research Association [AERA], 2003). The benefits were greatest for minority students and those on free lunch.

Although many studies conclude that smaller classroom sizes can produce small (but statistically significant) gains in performance on standardized test scores (Glass and Smith, 1979; Glass et al., 1982; Molnar, 1999; Bohrnstedt and Stecher, 2002), adoption of class-size-reduction policies has not always resulted in improved performance, due to the lack of high-quality teachers to fill the increased slots (Bohrnstedt and Stecher, 2002). This gives a warning that adoption of policies without attention to factors such as labor-market forces can be deleterious to those the policies were intended to serve. Other analysis of the California policy indicated it was very costly relative to the improvements gained (Brewer et al., 1999).

Evidence That Training Matters

The teacher-quality literature provides some (mixed) quasi-experimental evidence indicating that teacher training can improve student academic outcomes. In a quasi-experimental study of in-service teacher pedagogical skills for language and math, students whose teachers received specific training had significantly improved scores compared to students with teachers not subject to the training (Angrist and Lavy, 1998). However, modest levels of training may be insufficient in high-poverty areas (Jacob and Lefgren, 2002). In Chicago, a quasi-experimental design that took advantage of school-reform efforts that included in-service training for teachers showed that marginal increases in in-service training did not have a significant impact on student reading or math achievement. Thus, while there is evidence that in some cases, teacher training can produce better student outcomes, this may not apply when the level of training is very modest or occurs in schools with significant challenges.

In carrying these findings over to the OST field, one must be cautious. They can primarily be used to caution providers about how they probably should consider carefully the types and levels of training for staff, perhaps experimenting with it carefully to determine what combinations produce the best results. It is an open question, given the above, whether staff training can produce student academic improvements when it involves poorly educated staff such as those that characterize many OST programs.

Converging Evidence on Program Factors Associated with Positive Outcomes

Looking across the three broad literatures that consider what characteristics of a program are positively associated with higher-quality school-age-care, youth-development, or education outcomes in OST programs, we emphasize that the evidence in this area is heavily dependent on correlation studies and expert opinion. The evidence, when taken as a whole, however, does point to common program factors that may promote positive youth outcomes, as shown in Table 5.4.

All three literatures emphasize the importance of providing an environment that is physically and psychologically safe and orderly. The youth-development and education literatures both emphasize the importance of having high expectations of youth, be it with respect to their conduct, learning, or achievement. The school-age-care and youth-development literatures highlight the need to offer opportunities that are age-appropriate and challenging, that provide opportunities to develop or master new skills, and that emphasize the importance of trying to integrate community, program, and family efforts to support youth, including coordination with formal schools, use of volunteers, and community services and organizations. The school-age-care and education literatures each mention two quality characteristics, which, of all the indicators, have the strongest empirical support: limiting the size of the program or classroom and staff or teacher training. Additionally, both the school-age-care and education literatures emphasize the importance of having clear objectives and frequent assessment of how and whether the organization is achieving its objectives.

Implications

This convergence of multiple, but not rigorous studies, points to the following program factors that have been at least loosely associated with positive youth outcomes and are congruent with different standards that have been proposed for OST provision:

Table 5.4
Program Indicators Supported by at Least Two of the Three Literatures, by Literature

Youth Development	School-Age Care	Education
Physical and psychological safety	Attention to safety and health	Safe, orderly school environment
Positive social norms		High expectations for student achievement
Supportive relationships	Supportive emotional climate	
Opportunities for skill building	Age-appropriate activities	Opportunity to learn
Appropriate structure		Strong instructional leadership
Integration of family, school, and community efforts	Continuity and complementarity with day school programs	Constructive home and school relations
	Positive family involvement	
	Use of volunteers	
	Community partnerships	
	Small total enrollment	Small classroom size
	Trained staff	Trained teachers
	Clear goals and evaluation of program	Clear mission
		Frequent assessment of academic progress

- a clear mission
- high expectations and positive social norms
- a safe and healthy environment
- a supportive emotional climate
- a small total enrollment
- stable, trained personnel
- appropriate content and pedagogy relative to the children's needs and the program's mission, with opportunities to engage
- integrated family and community partners
- frequent assessment.

We propose this list as a set of program components that are likely, although certainly not proven, to produce more effective group-based

OST programming. There are several efforts underway to further identify quality indicators for OST programming to provide more conclusive and useful results than provided in this chapter. To our knowledge, these efforts at best involve further correlation research. For example, one such proposed study will take programs nominated by experts as having high quality and identifying common distinguishing features among this group. This approach is similar to the early effective-schools literature described in this chapter. While such efforts could help further elaborate the lists laid out in this chapter, the findings will be no more conclusive.

We close this chapter with a call for more rigorous assessment of what components of a program work to increase participant benefits. However, we caveat this call with the observation that testing specific program features is very rare in other fields because one usually wants to know whether the whole program works before looking at individual components. Testing components tends to be even more complicated and costly than testing an entire program.

Decision makers should step back and think seriously about how to test specific program features. One might want to take lists of program components, such as those laid out here or elsewhere, as a starting point for designing programs. Those programs could be evaluated, and those found to be effective could be examined more closely for the relative importance of individual program components. This approach can have high payoff if accompanied by detailed cost analysis because it could provide the means to find the combinations of factors that more cost-effectively ensure the desired results.

CHAPTER SIX

Improving Participation in OST Programs

In Chapter Three we noted that the supply of OST programs exceeds demand. Chapters Four and Five highlight some of the potential reasons why—a paucity of effective programs and a fledgling understanding of what constitutes quality. If one is optimistic and assumes that the field can move forward in developing and delivering effective, quality programming, then decision makers and providers would want to turn their attention to attracting participants to programs. To ensure this long-term goal, programs need to be both effective at achieving desired objectives and attractive and available to target participants.

In this chapter, we examine what is known about how people, especially children and youth, make decisions about program participation. We draw from several literatures to explore the issue of how to increase participation, assuming that this emphasis is justified. We include the well-established and scientifically confirmed understanding of how people generally decide to participate in voluntary activities from the general psychology literature. We access specific applications from applied fields such as military recruiting and recruiting for job-training programs. This information lays the groundwork for how to design and market programs that are attractive to target population.

We note that our review showed few studies that directly measure these issues within OST settings. We know virtually nothing about whether and how these ideas specifically relate to school-age children and adolescents deciding to participate in OST programs. For example, while psychologists and market researchers have established that attitudes and environmental barriers are key to understanding one's decision-making process, we know very little about the attitudes youth hold with respect to specific OST programs.

In this chapter we first cover what is specifically known about participation in OST activities. We then describe what the psychology field reveals about factors that enable or offer barriers to participation. Next we look at practical applications for programs in related fields. We then draw out implications.

We find in general that while interesting but not always proven ideas abound about how to improve participation in other fields, little has been published about how to improve participation in this field, and much work remains to be done.

Patterns of Participation in OST Activities

Previous discussion in this volume provided some information about the level of participation in OST activities. Review of four nationally representative surveys of youth and how they spend their time indicate who is most likely to be involved in OST activities (Quinn, 1999; Hofferth and Sandberg, 2001; Smith et al., 2002; DOEd, 2004). We note that each survey looked at slightly different subpopulations. For example, Hofferth and Sandberg (2001) examined grades K–8, while Smith et al. (2002) examined ages 10–18 and church-based youth programs. The following summarizes the results of these surveys.

- Children with the following types of characteristics tend to be overrepresented in after-school programs serving children in grades K–8: children with a single parent, children from two-parent families where the mother works, black children, non-Hispanic children, and younger children. In addition, of eighth-graders, higher-income children are overrepresented and lower-income children are underrepresented in out-of-school activities. Finally, of children 10–18 years old, children with two parents with mothers who do not work, black children, and younger children are overrepresented in church youth groups.
- Some groups are underrepresented in after-school programs—for example, children from two-parent families with mothers who do not work, white children, non-Hispanic children, and older youth. Of eighth-graders, children from lower-income families

are underrepresented in out-of school programs. Finally, of children 10–18 years old, Hispanic children and older children are underrepresented in church youth groups.

The patterns revealed are likely to reflect demographic and cultural differences in attitudes, knowledge or awareness, and resources. In no case are youth in the same group always more likely to participate in OST programs; rather, it depends on the particular type of program. For example, youth in single-parent households and two-parent households with a working mother are more likely to participate in after-school programs than youth in a household structure of two parents where the mother is not employed. Children in those families are more likely to participate in religious activities than other types of activities. Black youth are more likely to participate in after-school center-based programs and religious activities, while white youth are more likely than other youth to participate in sports activities, which are often school-related. Hispanic youth are no more likely to engage in any of these activities than other youth (although they fall somewhere in between black and white youth in participation rates in center-based after-school programs).

With the exception of extracurricular activities (e.g., band, orchestra, hobby clubs) there is only limited evidence that income is positively related to participation in after-school activities (Zill, Nord, and Loomis, 1995). This might reflect the fact that some of these programs are subsidized (in particular after-school programs) and that, as some have argued, lower-income families enroll more often in subsidized programs or slots (Halpern, 1999).

As seen in Chapter Four, researchers note that there is a correlation between the age of the student and attendance: the older the student is, the clearer the drop-off in attendance (Hofferth et al., 1991; Vandell and Shumow, 1999; Grossman et al., 2002; DOEd, 2003). Moreover, there is a steady decline in attendance through the school year.

Factors Important in Promoting Participation

In this section, we describe the key dimensions of the decision-making process that have been validated by behavioral theorists and applied researchers as effecting behavior change in other fields (such as health care). We draw from a recent report produced by a National Institutes of Health committee convened to study effective interventions to prevent HIV risk behaviors (Fishbein 2000; Fishbein et al. 2001). We describe how this knowledge of behavior can be used to develop strategies to increase participation in OST programs.

Researchers have established that three main factors influence decisions: motivations, intentions, and environmental factors. In general, the way behavioral theorists and applied researchers think about making a decision to do something is a combination of positive attitudes (i.e., a person believes it is desirable to do something), strong intent, and lack of environmental barriers that could impede acting on the intent. Environmental barriers include issues such as lack of transportation or the high costs of program attendance.

It is generally assumed that identifying and addressing these environmental barriers to participation will be sufficient to engage children and youth in OST programs. Behavioral theorists, however, argue that removing these barriers does not create motivation and intention. As described below, empirical evidence exists from several studies to document the existence of environmental barriers to enroll and attend in OST programs. However, surprisingly little is known about motivation and intent to participate in these programs.

Environmental Factors Associated with Participation

Most of research and practitioner efforts at improving participation in OST activities focus on reducing environmental barriers. Researchers have identified three types of barriers: information and awareness, scheduling of activities, and access, including cost.

- Lack of information about available OST opportunities can prevent participation. Parents and children are not always aware of the many opportunities available to them in the nonschool hours (Hobbs, 1999; Halpern, Spielberger, and Rob, 2001).
- Another practical barrier is scheduling (Heaviside et al., 1995; Zill, Nord, and Loomis, 1995; Halpern, Speilberger, and Rob, 2001; DOEd, 2003). Participation is influenced by the time

when the activity takes place and whether this schedule fits with the youth's other activities and obligations (such as supervising a sibling or doing household chores).

- Access constraints, especially those resulting from cost and transportation, have been identified as especially important and factor heavily in low-income families (Hustman, 1992; Seppanen et al., 1993; DOEd, 2003; Duffett and Johnson, 2004). Lower-income families face greater financial and physical barriers, including the absence of programs in their neighborhoods (Searle and Jackson, 1985; Littell and Wynn, 1989; Skillman Foundation, 1995; Duffett and Johnson, 2004).

The greater the number of and extent of environmental barriers, the less likely it is that youth will participate in OST programs, assuming they intended to do so. Barriers can vary among programs. For example, the barriers to attending a local 21st CCLC after-school care program at a local elementary school are very different from those to attending an after-school art class at the local YMCA that is a bus ride away from either school or home. The barriers to the school-based program involve getting transportation from school to home after school lets out, which is a much less daunting process than coming up with the fee to participate in the YMCA program and getting from school to the YMCA to home.

Although these barriers can sometimes seem insurmountable, they are easy to identify and address with sufficient resources. Programs might be able to increase participation by targeting or removing barriers; for example, they can extend hours, reduce costs, or provide reliable, safe, affordable transportation.

Motivation and Intention Factors Associated with Participation

Experience and evidence from other areas, such as military recruiting, sports and leisure activities, and the arts, indicate that the percentage of the eligible population that has made the decision to participate is dwarfed by the number of persons who have yet to form an intent to do so. To understand the importance of intent and motivation, consider the following estimates from military-recruiting literature: 70 percent of male high-school seniors who said they were strongly inclined to join the military within six years did, compared with 30 percent of those moderately inclined and 6 percent of those who said they definitely would not join (Buchmann, 2002). If someone has a strong intention to do something, they are likely to do it unless there are environmental barriers or they lack the skills to undertake it.

Behavioral theorists (summarized in NRC, 2003), identify the following factors as positively strengthening intention to participate: clearly perceived benefits, lack of competing activities, support from key influencers, and positive program experiences. We cover each in turn.

Clearly perceived benefits. People are more likely to intend to participate in an activity that they believe will benefit them. Similarly, if a person believes that an activity will produce undesirable results, then the person is less likely to participate. It also matters how much value the person places in the positive or negative outcome. For example, if youth think that doing something will please their parents, and they highly value pleasing parents, then they are likely to have a strong intent to engage in this activity over one that is less likely to please their parents. This implies recruiting efforts should consider developing program content and advertising that focuses on benefits important to the target population and should communicate the potential of these benefits to the target population.

Lack of benefits from competing activities. Besides considering the benefits (and costs) of engaging in a specific behavior when making decisions, people also jointly consider trade-offs with the perceived benefits and costs of alternative or competing activities. When trying to figure out ways to improve a group's attitudes toward, and intention to engage in, an activity, it is important to understand the value of competing activities to youth. Providers can then fashion a message that emphasizes the unique benefits of the program activities or structure the program such that the perceived competition is diminished.

Supportive key influencers. Key influencers can bring to bear social pressure on a youth to participate or not participate in certain behaviors. This works in two ways. First, youth can feel social pressure based on whether they believe that someone in their social network (family or friends) or even society at large thinks that they should or should not participate. In some families, a child may not be able to participate because of a parent's inability or unwillingness to support the participation (Hustman, 1992; Hobbs, 1999; Halpern, 2000) or because of cultural or other reasons. Second, youth might believe that important influencers engage or do not engage in the activity. In other words, both "do as I do" and "do as I say" appear to influence the total amount of social pressure one believes is exerted by key influencers.

Peers are especially important in teen years. Developmental psychologists have identified adolescence, especially early adolescence, as a critical period when the social pressure exerted by peers is the most powerful (NRC and IOM, 2002). Although it is open to debate whether peers are as important as parents at this age, it is clear that what youth think their peers are thinking and doing is more important starting around age 12 or 13 than at earlier ages, and that while the impact of social pressure will decrease by late adolescence, it will still remain stronger than it was in childhood.

Thus, in designing a way to increase participation of adolescents in OST programs, it might be important to understand the parents' relative attitudes, norms, and self-efficacy with respect to enrolling children in a program and to understand peers' attitudes toward participation in the activity.

Positive program experiences. The above factors all can influence a child to attend, but unless attendance produces a positive experience, participation will decrease. Thus, positive program experiences provide a feedback loop to encourage greater participation. OST programs can influence the attitudes that targeted youth have about the program by ensuring that the actual experience of those who show up is positive.

Lack of Data on Attitudes about OST Opportunities for Target Populations

As shown above, understanding youth attitudes or perceptions toward specific OST programs is critical to determining how to effectively recruit and retain participants. Currently, most efforts to assess attitudes toward OST programs focus on public-opinion polls as the means of gauging public support for increased public funding of these programs and not on understanding the attitudes and beliefs of those the programs are intended to serve.

We found only one study that formally assessed youth's views of the program. As part of the 21st CCLC (DOEd, 2003), middle-school nonparticipants and participants (and their parents) were surveyed about their views of 21st CCLC. Nonparticipants were asked under what circumstances they would participate in the after-school program. Middle-school nonparticipants said they would go if they could choose what they did there (81 percent), if more of their friends went there (78 percent), if it were less like school (67 percent), or if they could get their homework done there (67 percent). In turn, participants' most frequently reported perceptions of the centers were as a good place for getting your homework done (87 percent) and a fun place for anyone to go (86 percent).

While this type of survey recognizes the importance of positive and negative perceptions that influence youth's (and parents') decisions about OST activities, it also shows, as applied behavioral theorists know, that the role of perceptual factors is more complicated and hinges on perceptions about a particular activity and perceptions of alternative activities.

This view is further supported by the work of Lauver, Little, and Weiss (2004). In their follow-up survey of program evaluations that examined participation, respondents identified what they understood to be the important factors in determining whether youth participated. Barriers to participation included the desire to relax and hang out with friends after school, the desire or need to work, family responsibilities, boredom or disinterest, and transportation and safety factors.

A recent telephone survey of parents and children by Duffett and Johnson (2004) confirmed these results. According to the children surveyed, lack of motivation was the most likely reason for not participating in organized after school activities (71 percent of youth respondents). Other reasons cited were that the programs were too expensive (29 percent) or that programs were too far away (28 percent).

In other words, if getting homework done is a valued outcome of youths, then to ensure participation a program will need to be perceived as at least as good a place to complete homework as other alternatives.

In addition, getting homework done must be as desired an outcome as others, such as sports, band, or hanging out, to ensure participation. These values likely vary across different groups, for different outcomes, and even for different OST activities.

Thus, the key challenge that has not been systematically undertaken in this field, as far as we could uncover, is understanding the attitudes that youth hold toward specific OST programs and how these attitudes compare with attitudes the same youth hold toward alternatives to those programs. Without this, it will be difficult to increase participation. At the same time, one needs to recognize that attitudes are likely to reflect at least partial realities of OST programs. To the extent that future programs are designed and implemented of to be more effective and higher quality, attitudes may be altered to reflect this barring any stigmatization (which can plague even the best-designed social program).

Lessons from Practical Efforts to Increase Enrollment

In addition to findings based on behavioral theory, lessons from efforts to increase participation in job-training programs and to promote military enlistment also provide practical ideas that can be applied to recruiting in the OST field.

Guidance from the Job-Training and Military-Enlistment Fields on Increasing Enrollment

Although participation in job-training programs is generally required for receipt of cash assistance, job-training programs usually have a difficult time engaging a large proportion of welfare caseloads. The Manpower Demonstration Research Corporation (MDRC) prepared a book summarizing best practices and advice for achieving higher participation levels in job-training programs (Hamilton and Scrivener, 1999). Some of the best practices are based on empirical research across programs assessing outcomes, whereas others are based on program experience not tied to outcomes. We recognize that there are other fields that have paid considerable attention to inducing participation, and there are certainly lessons to be learned, such as those relating to participation in preventive and therapeutic interventions. To limit the scope of this section, we purposely restrict ourselves to the job-training literature because it is similar to OST programs in two key ways: it is a subsidized program, and its target population (adolescents and adults) at least partially overlaps with the target population of some OST programs. Below, we present those practices that are grounded in empirical research and that might be applicable to recruiting in the OST field.

All possible participants. A successful outreach effort means that potential participants are both aware of the program and the opportunities presented by participating in the program. Thus, the first step toward increased participation is ensuring that all potential participants are identified and that they or their guardians are aware of the program and its potential benefits.

Resources for outreach and recruitment. Within the OST literature, we find support for the importance of recruiting and outreach and the need to allocate significant resources to it. Specifically, the experiences of providers in the ESS initiative suggest that providers can increase awareness of programs with families by sending out mailings to households, holding open houses at the school, providing materials in multiple languages, and holding registration at areas where youth families congregate, such as housing complexes (Grossman et al., 2002). They also note that high-needs youth might require more aggressive outreach (Grossman et al., 2002).

Some job-training programs that had successful outreach efforts dedicated a staff person as "case finder" who was devoted to reviewing the status of welfare recipients and determining whether they should be in the program (Hamilton and Scrivener, 1999).

The military relies heavily on recruiters for identifying and converting potential recruits (i.e., moving those with a high propensity to participate into the participation stage by providing information). Recruiters use a variety of methods for identifying leads (e.g., displays at high schools, responses from local ads, referrals from other applicants, and posters set up in businesses). The Armed Services believe that interactive Web sites are a very effective way to identify potential recruits (NRC, 2003).

Location. Some argue that the best way to generate more enlistees is to locate where youth and their key influencers (e.g., parents) congregate (Fricker and Fair, 2003). Because recruiters' time is finite and they cannot pursue more leads using traditional methods, the military is experimenting with "marketing-enhanced" recruiting stations. Bringing recruiting stations that also serve as marketing stations into high-volume places where youth and adult influencers are made aware of and can freely obtain information on the services has so far shown mixed results (Fricker and Fair, 2003).

Combining advertising budgets. Because advertising is expensive, the Department of Defense (DoD) is experimenting with using a DoD-wide advertising effort to promote the military rather than service-specific advertising. The effectiveness of this approach in generating demand across all military services is not known (Dertouzos and Garber, 2003). The ambiguity of the conclusions likely means that at worst a general military advertising strategy is not substantially less effective than service-specific advertising and is potentially considerably more cost-effective.

Guidance from the Job-Training and Military-Enlistment Fields on Increasing Attendance

As noted above, not only is it hard to recruit youth into OST programs, it is also hard to keep them in the programs once they have enrolled in them. The job-training and military-enlistment fields offer some practical guidance on how to increase retention within programs.

Attendance and follow-up. Practices that were effective in monitoring and encouraging ongoing participation in job-training programs included using moderate or intensive monitoring (Hamilton and Scrivener, 1999). Monitoring effectiveness depends on the amount of time and effort staff can spend on monitoring, the quality of an automated monitoring system, and the priority placed on monitoring by the program (or funders). In other words, effective monitoring means ensuring that staff has the time to monitor participation, that a well-designed tracking system is in place (which can be costly), and that monitoring is made a priority.

The cost of ongoing monitoring and outreach can be expensive. In QOP, a comprehensive case-management program for high-school students, the one site (of five) that was responsible for almost all the overall program's success took this approach, some would argue, to extremes (Maxfield, Schirm, and Rodriguez-Planas, 2003). QOP identified youth to enroll in the program, and then the youth worker assigned to each youth was tasked with engaging the youth, whether they quit, moved, or never engaged. The cost per youth at this site was $49,000 for five years, largely because of the extensive outreach recruitment and retention effort. If resources are limited, a program might consider identifying those youth who are likely to benefit the most from participating and intentionally devote resources to monitoring (and retaining) them.

Incentives to the program for attendance. Job-training experiences indicate that the use of financial sanctions (or rewards) can be useful. In the case of job-training experiences, sanctioning occurs at two levels: participants and programs. It is difficult to think of how sanctions could be applied to participants in OST, but one can think about incentives to participation. QOP, the case-management youth-development program described above, was unique in that it paid youth $1.25 per hour of participation (called allowances). While allowances were a major cost component of the program, the impact of allowances on participation and program outcomes has not been analyzed. Nor has such an approach been used in group-based OST programs.

Programs can be sanctioned if they fail to achieve prespecified goals. To the extent that it is important that participants maintain a minimum level of attendance (e.g., because a certain level is required before benefits accrue), the use of financial sanctions (or incentives) for programs that meet certain participation goals can provide incentives to achieve those goals using the methods they find most effective in for target populations. (Of course, if financial incentives or sanctions are used, programs will need to be audited to make sure that the rates they report are not inflated.)

Implications

The chapter assumes that programs offer a valued net benefit to participants, when compared to program nonparticipants. That is a major unproven assumption. Given the assumption that OST programming improves to the point that youth can significantly benefit from participation, it would be useful to focus on targeting youth to participate and to ensure attendance at a sufficiently high level to benefit.

We conclude that much work needs to be done to better understand how to build programs that youth would want to attend, and that, should policymakers decide that increasing participation is an important objective, significant resources would have to be devoted to the effort to make it effective in targeting specific populations. This review offers practices from other fields that providers could implement now that might improve their participation, if carefully and thoughtfully adapted.

National or Regional Surveys

Future research could focus on clarifying and identifying ways to effectively intervene to strengthen intention of individuals to engage in OST activities. In particular, survey data would be helpful in understanding perceived benefits of specific types of OST programs, the key influencers with respect to OST participation and how supportive these key influencers are, and the perceived benefits of alternative uses of OST. This type of information—about beliefs, values, and attitudes—needs to be collected for major classes of youth (such as low-income, immigrant, minority, low-achieving, and at-risk) to provide reasonably accurate views of what broad segments of the youth population are looking for in OST activities and what will encourage their participation.

Such data-collection efforts could be undertaken nationally or in specific geographic areas. To reduce costs they could easily be piggybacked on existing and routine survey efforts, including the National Household Education Surveys (NHES) or Monitoring the Future, a national annual survey of the behaviors, attitudes, and values of American secondary-school students. Public reports should provide program designers and decision makers with information on factors to consider in designing appealing (as well as effective) programs. Because this type of information would benefit multiple users, partnerships of providers, foundations, and government could usefully help defray the burden of costs.

The data-collection effort can be used to design coordinated messages or selling points for youth and parents that are intended to improve attitudes of intended users and their key influencers towards these programs, as well as create content that is needed and appealing. Specific programs and local decision makers could piggyback on these messages or tailor them for their constituencies.

Program-Level Campaigns

An OST program would want to identify members of the program's target population and provide outreach. Ideally, outreach would include "marketing" the program—that is, shaping positive attitudes held about the program, identifying and overcoming barriers to participation, and generally encouraging the formation of an intent to participate. The message from the above literature is that this process should be thorough and should use multiple sources. For example, principals, teachers, aides, librarians, bus drivers, and counselors, as well as parents of children who are already involved, can help identify and recruit potential participants and sell the program. Outreach should also be conducted in multiple places and times that parents and children tend to congregate on a regular basis, such as during back-to-school nights or parent-teacher conferences, or at local community organizations (such as libraries or recreation centers), churches and faith-based organizations, local welfare agencies, or housing centers.

Lessons from the military suggest that community-based programs in a local area can consider banding together to develop a targeted advertising message or approach. Multiple programs can cooperate in setting up stations or kiosks in high-volume areas where they can generate interest in OST programs and speak with prospective participants and key influencers. Such locales include retail malls, local fairs, or parks.

Finally, once a program has attracted a participant, maintaining attendance should become a focus through continuously monitoring attendance (which some organizations can do using keycards) and then assiduously following up with youth whose attendance falls off. This way a program can immediately identify and rectify any problems under its control, such as transportation issues, cost, or interpersonal problems involving staff or other participants. Providing incentives to the participant or program itself for maintaining high rates of attendance might work, though this can be costly if the incentives are financial. If the program itself is to receive incentives (or disincentives for decline in attendance rates), then a system needs to be established whereby the funding stream itself is tied in some way to actual participation (and continually monitored).

CHAPTER SEVEN

Capacity Building

In the last chapter we discussed how the field could work to build participation in programs, should that prove to be a worthwhile goal. In this chapter, we address what is known about how to build the capacity in the provider community to provide quality programming. While the exact nature of demand for OST services remains uncertain at all levels, how to build the capacity to provide better and more complete service-delivery systems is of interest to policymakers in the arena.

Linnell defines *capacity* as "an organization's ability to achieve its mission effectively and to sustain itself over the long-term. Capacity also refers to the skills and capabilities of individuals" (2004, p. 1). Linnell defines *capacity building* as "activities that improve an organization's ability to achieve its mission"(2004, p. 1). Backer simply refers to capacity building as "strengthening nonprofits so they can better achieve their mission" (2000, p. 8).

Wynn (2000) provides a rationale for why the issue of capacity building has arisen in the OST field. She argues that while the organizations that serve youth outside of school hours are varied, they face, as a group, a set of common challenges: "These challenges include the absence of a clear mandate regarding their primary function; the lack of program standards and substantial variation in program quality; a host of operations impediments related to facilities, staffing, administrative supports, and financing; and the need for identified outcomes and an attention to accountability for achieving them" (p. 4).

Her problem statement for the field has been echoed by others, but perhaps with different issues emphasized. For example, Halpern (2002) emphasizes poor-quality staff and staff turnover as major impediments to quality provision. Halpern and others (Tolman et al., 2002; Pittman, Wilson-Ahlstrom, and Yohalem, 2003) also focus on the fragmented nature of the existing providers and call for greater "systems building," by which they mean increased interrelationships and interdependence among providers, clients, funders, and the larger community to ensure a more coherent and more regular pattern of services to meet needs. VanderWood used the term *system change* as "getting the best practices or innovative ideas accepted, generating or redirecting the resources needed to support them for the long-term, and then imbedding these new methods in the regular 'business as usual' practices of government and service delivery systems" (2003, p. 6).

While capacity-building efforts have been at work in the nonprofit field for decades, it has not been systematically reviewed or culled for lessons (Backer, 2003).

This chapter first reviews the nature of the literature in this area. It discusses possible means to improve individual providers and then examines what we know about how to build system capacity and infrastructure across the whole field. As we will discuss next, the literature and level of investigation in this field is such that we cannot make recommendations about what should be done to build capacity in the field. But this review provides at least some lessons about what types of processes, tools, and approaches might prove useful in understanding how to go about determining what capacity building might encompass.

Nature of the Literature

In general the literature in this area is not only less rigorous from an evidentiary base than that covered in Chapters Four through Six, but it is also scant. The literature appears to fall into three categories, as shown in Table 7.1. First, there is literature on organizational effectiveness as applied to nonprofits based primarily on theoretical, general, or case-study observations. Second, there have been a series of studies done of OST programs and how they grew. Third, studies of related fields on early childhood provision, including Head Start, offer some

Table 7.1
Literature on Capacity Building

Literatures	Work	Quality
Organizational effectiveness for nonprofits		Theoretical
	Grossman, 1999	
	Backer, 2003	Reflective essay
	Backer, 2000	Synthesis and cross-site comparisons
Studies of OST	Forum for Youth Investment, 2003	Analysis
	Tolman et al., 2002	Analysis
	Wynn, 2000	Cross-site observations
	Governor's Crime Commision, 1998	Cross-site observations
	Halpern, 2002	Case study
	VanderWood, 2003	Case study
Related fields	Beckett, 2002, 2003	Historical analysis
	Zigler and Muenchow, 1992	Historical analysis
	Stoney, 1998	Policy analysis
	Schumacher, Irish and Lombardin, 2003	Policy analysis

historical insights into capacity-building challenges. Finally, there have been a series of reflective essays on the field and where it is headed, calling for a series of actions. Because of the nature of this literature as a whole, we draw very limited implications.

Improving Individual Providers

Three theoretical syntheses provided some insights into the challenges faced in improving the capacity of individual providers and some possible actions that could be taken.

Incentive Systems for Nonprofits

Allan Grossman (1999) reviews the systems of motives and incentives that act on nonprofits and concludes that they are generally not motivated to improve effectiveness, and therefore are not motivated to build capacity. First, he notes that philanthropic funders in America generally cover start-up costs for nonprofit providers, but tend not to cover operating costs or capital-investment costs, thus providing an inadvertent incentive for providers to always remain in a start-up phase. Second, providers who are unsuccessful in establishing a strong financial footing are more likely to continue to receive philanthropic funding, as the funders do not wish to cut off services to indigent populations. Meanwhile, those providers that do manage to find a strong financial footing, say through charging fee-for-services, will find funding from foundations cut. This system again provides an incentive to providers to not search for ways to provide a strong financial basis for their operations. Third, the philanthropic community itself is very fragmented, with each individual foundation or philanthropist having their specific program emphases that change periodically. Also, funding grants can be quite small or for short periods of time as funders seek to maintain some control over spending. This leads to a system where providers must spend inordinate amounts of managerial time pursuing client relationships to maintain a funding stream. Fourth, Grossman observes that providers sometimes find themselves caught between the desires of the funders and the needs and desires of the client base. The two are often not the same, and this dynamic can lead to poor service provision from the point of view of the client. Finally, funders do not adequately monitor providers to ensure high-quality provision, again leaving open the door to poor service provision.

Grossman (1999) observes that not only does this current system of relationships between funders, providers, and clients offer few incentives to build capacity and organizational effectiveness, but unless it is significantly changed, the organizational effectiveness of providers will remain low. He argues for the adoption of capital-venture approaches, such as those in the current marketplace for charter schools and educational improvements, where venture-capitalists reward providers with further capital for improvements and expansion when they offer exemplary services. He notes that several capital-venture approaches are being taken now within the philanthropic field and should be studied to understand if this approach provides better incentives for improved performance within the nonprofit service sector. In short, improvement efforts must include a changed relationship with increased assessment and accountability between the funders and providers.

Role of Foundations

At the behest of the John S. and James L. Knight Foundation, the Human Interaction Research Institute (Backer, 2000) undertook an environmental scan of capacity-building efforts in philanthropy that included interviews with leaders and technical experts in the field, a literature review, and a review of current efforts in the field. From these sources it drew some conditions or characteristics of effective capacity-building programs sponsored or operated by foundations. Note that this analysis was not tied to any specific outcome indicators. We paraphrase the effective characteristics here (p. 4):

- *Comprehensive.* The more impactful activities offered "one-stop-shopping" in which grantees could access a range of assessment services, technical assistance, and financial and other kinds of support.
- *Customized.* Capacity-building services are customized to the needs of the nonprofit and its environment.
- *Competence-based.* Capacity-building services are offered by well-trained providers and requested by informed consumers.
- *Timely.* Services are provided at an appropriate time and in an appropriate time frame to make a difference.
- *Peer-connected.* Opportunities are provided for networking, mentoring, and information sharing among providers.
- *Assessment-based.* Capacity begins with a thorough assessment of the needs and assets of the provider relative to the community.
- *Readiness-based.* The client is ready to receive and act upon the services.
- *Contextualized.* Capacity-building services are received in concert with a larger effort to improve services by the foundation, the provider and the community.

In later work, Backer uses the term "adaptive capacity" (2003, p. 2) to capture the need for nonprofits to monitor, access, and respond to the internal and external environments. Backer notes three major types of capacity building activities predominant in the nonprofit sector and supported largely by foundations (2000, pp. 8–10):

- *Assessment.* This involves effectively measuring the nonprofit's current needs and assets. Its readiness to undertake change is necessary to design and build an improvement effort.
- *Intervention.* Capacity building usually involves management consultation, training of staff, or technical assistance.
- *Direct financial support.* Capacity building usually demands funding for core operating support, specific capital grants for equipment or facilities, and working capital to stay afloat while payments are being processed.

Other types of actions might also be effective, including "improving the level and quality of strategic alliances; collaborating and networking with others in the community; increasing the extent to which nonprofits share knowledge with colleague organizations; and improving the ability of nonprofits to explicate their goals" in relation to their activities (Backer, 2003, p. 2).

Role of Intermediaries

At the behest of the Edna McConnell Clark Foundation, Wynn (2000) examined the role of local intermediaries in promoting and shaping a vision for youth development in general. Intermediaries work with provider organizations to improve their services, but are not funders. They act as "brokers and facilitators functioning both as representatives and agents of change" (p. 11). Chapter Two of this report noted the growth of these intermediaries in the last several years. Wynn classifies their major purposes as

- convening and networking
- knowledge development and dissemination
- standards identification and setting
- training
- management assistance
- advocacy and representation
- accountability.

She notes several successes in helping build better systems of providers within communities. But she also notes that intermediaries suffer from some of the same incentives issues identified by Grossman (1999).

Current Actions

Lest the reader believe that the field has not been active in promoting the improvement of individual providers along the lines described above, several examples of just such activities as prescribed have been completed or are underway.

- NIOST and NSACA have both produced standards for quality care provision, as mentioned in Chapter Five. These can be used by providers for self-assessment and for mission standards or by funders as a yardstick for progress toward better provision.
- Several organizations are now functioning in this arena, providing funding to nonprofits under market-based criteria for performance as suggested by Grossman. These include the Entrepreneur's Foundation, New Profits, the Roberts Enterprise Development Fund, and the Open Society Institute.
- The Edna McConnell Clark Foundation has supported moves in this direction by supporting better management function and assessment and accountability approaches through use of tools it has helped to develop.
- The Finance Project, the Harvard Family Research Project, NIOST, and NSACA have provided technical assistance to providers in the areas of finance, content development, staff development, and standard accreditation to strengthen the capacity of existing providers to offer quality services.

Summary

In summing up this literature, we would say that there are strong arguments that the capacity of individual providers can be improved through comprehensive, timely, and coordinated assistance based on systematic assessments of needs and assets relative to the community. Case studies of specific efforts have concluded that sharing, networking, and collaboration among providers and the community resulted in some providers able to offer improved services, better staff training, more stable resources, and better evaluation of progress. But better provision might also be forthcoming if incentives between providers and funders change to emphasize the use of performance-based assessment and accountability. Because much of the evidence in regard to these types of solutions is not well documented or studied, we conclude that while promising and commonsensical, these ideas are not proven. Actors should consider and undertake them with reasonable caution and realistic expectations for results.

Building System Capacity

While progress in improving services might be accomplished simply by intervening with individual providers as indicated above, some argue that more systemic approaches might be taken (Halpern, 2002; Tolman et al., 2002; Pittman, Wilson-Ahlstrom, and Yohalem, 2003).

Local Level

Sometimes this is argued from a local level. For example, the Governor's Crime Commission (1998) *After-School Program Handbook: Strategies and Effective Practices* provides examples of how communities have maintained ongoing support for their programs. These examples are organized into several areas, such as providing recognition to programs supporters, involving parents more directly, promoting the programs through media events, forming collaborations and partnerships, conducting fund-raising events, diversifying funding sources, and developing long-range community plans. In addition, the Robert Wood Johnson Foundation funded the development of local system-building approaches in five cites and has sponsored evaluations of those efforts (VanderWood, 2003). But, as Halpern points out in his review of two system-building efforts at the local level, "the very idea of an after-school system remains difficult to bring into focus. The way of looking at and thinking about after-school systems that I have proposed needs debate, argument, and revision, as does my conceptualization of system building tasks" (2002, p. 23).

National-Level Program Development

Others argue from the national level and are especially concerned with ensuring program quality and a stable funding stream for programs. These include arguments for standards, federal funding, and the building of quality-assurance mechanisms (Tolman et al., 2002; Pittman, Wilson-Ahlstrom, and Yohalem, 2003) and are somewhat reminiscent of arguments heard over several decades during the development of the drug-prevention programs such as DARE and the early-childhood Head Start program.

Beckett (2002) argues that the history of the drug-prevention field highlights the importance of formal evaluation and self-improvement efforts in stabilizing an emerging field. Two decades ago, significant funds were funneled into school-based drug-prevention programs. Early but poorly designed evaluations showed that these programs were promising (see Clayton et al., 1991, for a review of these evaluations). Later rigorous evaluations came to the opposite conclusion. Programs like DARE had very little or no effect on drug use and the costs were not justified, thus threatening the funding streams for these programs (see U.S. General Accounting Office [GAO], 2003, for a summary of these evaluations).

Next-generation school-based drug-prevention programs were subsequently designed and rigorously assessed, and that many were found to effectively reduce substance use helped to confirm the value of these programs to policymakers who fund them (GAO, 2003). As a result, the federal government has pushed for adopting better-designed programs, like Project ALERT, that have rigorous evaluations and yield credible and positive results. DHHS and DOEd, along with other organizations, like the Promising Practices Network, have compiled lists of proven and recommended programs for schools wanting to implement these programs (for example, DOEd's Safe, Disciplined, and Drug-Free Schools Exemplary Programs).

This history has parallels to Head Start program growth. Head Start was begun during the Johnson administration as part of the Great Society War on Poverty in a time of flush budgets. It provided free education services to low-income preschool children to ensure that they would be ready for school. According to Zigler and Muenchow (1992), proponents at the time claimed that such programs would allow participants to increase their IQs, thus erasing any disadvantages that poverty-stricken youth might have relative to their more affluent peers when starting their formal education. Others argued that the program would ensure health-care provision, stronger motivation to achieve academically, and some basic skills sets in the participants.

Head Start did not have a rigorous evaluation, but nevertheless it gained very strong popular support and federal funding. Critics, however, have been skeptical of the program; the evaluations that have been done show significant variations in the quality of services provided across sites; and early evaluations showed insignificant learning on the part of participants, especially in the summer programs. One could argue that the lack of rigorous evaluation allowed the continued funding, because had the quality problems been made more concretely evident, funding would have collapsed. On the other hand, better evaluation early on might have been used to improve the program, guaranteeing stronger results for participants. Over time, the program administrators took steps to improve delivery—for example, by issuing standards for service provision, developing a quality-assurance system, and emphasizing more realistic and obtainable outcomes. The program is now for the first time undergoing a random-assignment experimental-design evaluation.

Zigler and Muenchow (1992) point to several lessons from this history. They emphasize the need for standards; for ongoing, rigorous evaluation and self-assessment; and for the active management of expectations among the interest groups and political sponsors involved.

Work by Stoney (1998) on behalf of the Horizons Initiative focuses on the multiple ways to finance an OST system by reviewing lessons from four fields (health, housing, higher education, and transportation) that might help those interested in improving services in the early-child-care field and ensuring more stable funding streams. Stoney's review describes several approaches, other than the creation of a permanent program, that might be considered, including the provision of subsidies or tax incentives, with the subsidy traveling with the child so the family can make decisions about the services provided; subsidies provided in the form of economic-development and investment policies to ensure the development of human and facilities capital; public investments in human capital; promotion of public-private partnerships to support accountability and quality assurance; further development of accountability mechanisms, such as has been done in the housing sector, where contractors are given rewards if housing is well maintained; and promoting private-sector involvement through leveraging their investments.

In a separate study, Schumacher, Irish, and Lombardi (2003) looked at how seven states attempted to improve early child-care provision through the use of program standards, technical assistance, monitoring, and contracting. The report shows how this approach, as compared to the more common licensing function of the states, ensured that the programs exceeded by far the minimal standards set by the state licensing board. The conclusion drawn is that state policies can help build the infrastructure and norms of provisions needed to strengthen the field.

In 1999, Project Grasp, an effort funded by the Mott Foundation and documented by the Forum for Youth Investment, supported four different cities in attempts to clarify and build strong support for an OST agenda. The report *Moving an Out-Of-School Agenda: Lessons and Challenges Across Cities* (Tolman et al., 2002) details ten steps that will have to be taken by cities to build a strong OST agenda and support for it. These steps are consistent with many of those proposed above. They include coordination, collaboration, and networking among organizations and stakeholders; building a stable and high-quality workforce; creating quality standards, assessments, and supports; developing the physical infrastructure; building leadership and political will; ensuring youth engagement; building public will and constituencies; developing plans and visions; and strengthening mapping, monitoring, and research.

In short, while many are calling for creation of permanent funding for specific programs like the 21st CLCC, others are posing more varied policy solutions to the challenge of system building.

Current Efforts

Efforts are underway by different actors to address systems building. Several examples provide some indication of the types of activities now taking place that might be considered capacity-building efforts at the system level and were covered in Chapter Two.

- The Edna McConnell Clark Foundation has funded the development and adoption of best practices under its Institution and Field Building Initiative.

- The Mott Foundation supports the Greater Resources for After-School Programming effort in four cities in partnership with the Forum for Youth Investment.
- The Wallace Foundation is providing assistance to efforts in New York City and Providence to build more integrated local approaches among providers.
- Foundations support and help maintain advocacy for sustained federal and state funding through support of the efforts of organizations like the Harvard Family Research Project, the Afterschool Alliance, and so on.

In addition, some have already incorporated the lessons from other fields concerning the need for standards, evaluations, and self-assessment. Pittman, Irby, and Ferber (2000) and Connell, Gambone, and Smith (2000) each note the importance of strengthening and interpreting the evidence base for programs. Gary Walker of Public/Private Ventures has outlined steps to improving the success of after-school provision, including a greater focus on evaluations and developing effective practices (Walker, 2004).

Implications

Our review indicated some thoughtful notions about how to improve and build capacity both of individual programs and across local, regional, and national markets. In the course of creating the review we also noted some of the examples of activities that have begun to spring up to accomplish these notions. In general, this review points to a few intriguing approaches that can be debated, but does not provide the evidence needed to create a well-crafted agenda.

- Strong arguments were uncovered that point to the effectiveness of more-integrated approaches, with collaboration, joint planning, and networking as important ways to further the debate as well as identifying shared challenges, best practices, and common interest among the groups involved.

- Historic examples reviewed showed the importance of evaluation, self-assessment, standards, and quality assurance to the development of other relevant fields.
- More-generic discussions pointed to the need for better incentives for improved performance and perhaps market-based relationships to engage competition as a way to increase performance. The predominant underlying system of poor incentives for performance and lack of accountability probably cannot form the base for an effective improvement effort.

Finally, given the level of the field, it seems prudent to think about local demonstrations of the types of system-building activities being advocated. If conducted with care and seriously evaluated with an eye toward gaining lessons, demonstrations could lead the way to better community infrastructure.

CHAPTER EIGHT

Conclusions

The purpose of this report was to systematically examine the research base for evidence that could help inform the growing public debate around subsidized, group-based OST programs. Specifically, we examined level of demand, program effectiveness, factors that might impact quality, determinants of participation, and possible practice to build capacity.

Findings and Implications

Our review of the literature in each of these areas resulted in the following findings and implications.

Level of Unmet Demand

Given the belief that demand outstrips supply, the current trend in the field is to push for capacity expansion, seeking to fund and provide more slots to meet the excess demand that has been widely asserted to exist.

In exploring the assertions of unmet demand, we could find little solid proof that it exists and, if so, what its nature is. Studies making such claims base them largely on the total number of children not being served in formal programs, not on an assessment of real unmet demand. At best these claims should be couched in the frame of "total possible demand." There was at least some evidence that many children are being cared for by relatives or others in their homes and do not choose, at least with the current offerings, to participate.

Furthermore, we found that programs that tracked enrollment and attendance are often undersubscribed and have low attendance.

We conclude that at this time it would be prudent of policymakers to be cautious about claims of broad unmet demand and the need to increase the quantity of slots and number of programs. Arriving at this conclusion will require a more formal assessment of what is being demanded and by whom, and what barriers to participation exist.

Effectiveness and Expectations for Outcomes
Any discussion of the future of OST needs to assess what can reasonably be expected from OST programs, at what cost, and for whom. Not only is it important to be clear about what types of impacts one expects from OST programming, but decision makers need to decide what size of impact they want to see, determine the practical means to achieve those levels, and then determine if those effect sizes merit the considerable funding involved, especially when compared to other options for using scarce public resources.

Claims of effectiveness of OST programs fall into four outcome areas: provision of school-age care, changed attitudes toward or actual changes in academic achievement and academic attainment, changed social and health behaviors, and changed social interactions.

Our review of the OST program evaluations found very few well-designed studies from which firm conclusions could be drawn. Even well-designed studies failed to account for the effect of participant's motivation on program participation, for participation level, or for implementation variation.

Analysis of the literature suggests that despite some of the extravagant claims by advocates, at best, some programs have produced modest positive effects in the following areas: educational expectations, high-school graduation rates, credits earned, attendance at postsecondary education, and social behaviors, such as reduced drug use or pregnancy. These program effects might vary by grade level, background of children, level of participation, program content and implementation quality, and whether the program developed was well targeted toward the desired outcome. In some cases, specific groups are more difficult to affect in OST settings.

In addition, we found that that the cost-effectiveness of these programs is not well understood or documented. In particular, we could find no studies that indicated the cost-benefit of an OST program relative to other options. This lack of cost-benefit information is combined with a lack of understanding of reasonable expectations of effects for the average attendance now predominant in OST programs. Fortunately, there is an emergence of interest in carefully collecting and reporting cost information. We encourage such efforts, especially those that attempt to capture all benefits and costs, identify the recipients or payers, and link costs and benefits in both the short and long term.

Policymakers would be well advised to be cautious and not overly optimistic about the effectiveness of OST programming as a panacea, even for provision of school-age care services. To achieve some of the expectations laid out (for example, in California's debates on Proposition 49) will take careful planning, attention, and significant funding. In addition, one needs to consider whether the effects now being achieved are worth the effort of a large social program (unless there are other important objectives). Before committing public funds to OST programming intended to raise academic achievement, as an example, one might want to compare its effectiveness to early childhood interventions, more uniform curriculum, better teacher-staff development, and so on.

Because so little is understood about the cost-effectiveness of these programs when compared to other options to meet the same objectives, policymakers should also be cautious about investing in these programs without better information on alternatives. These alternatives are available for educational goals, but perhaps less so for other objectives, such as prevention of risky behaviors.

Program Factors Associated with Quality

We examined evidence from several different fields to understand what program factors have been associated with quality provision. In general this literature is relatively weak empirically, without strong controls or random assignment. Nevertheless, we found converging evidence that nine factors are associated with quality program provision: (1) a clear mission; (2) high expectations and positive social norms expected of participants; (3) a safe and healthy environment; (4) a supportive emotional climate; (5) a small total enrollment; (6) stable, trained personnel; (7) appropriate content and pedagogy, relative to the children's needs and the program's mission, with opportunities to engage; (8) integrated family and community partners; and (9) frequent assessments.

While not fully substantiated by more rigorous research methods, these factors have a great deal of prima facie support and seem sensible. Thus, its seems prudent that any discussion involving improving provision would support implementation of these types of factors. Indeed, standards that have been promulgated by different advocacy and interest groups in the field support these factors.

Many of these qualities would take considerable resources and time to accomplish. For example, classroom-size reductions are costly and have had negative impacts when implemented in markets with a shortage of qualified personnel. Training of personnel can be costly and must be developed and delivered to support the goals of the program. Depending on the goals of the program, development of age-appropriate content, especially for programs with goals of seriously affecting achievement outcomes, might be expensive and well outside of the expertise levels of current OST program staff.

Decision makers and program implementers responsible for overseeing the quality of large OST programs are in an excellent position to further our understanding about what works and does not work. When rolling out a new practice, module, or program requirement, they can test its effect (and cost) in a sample of sites before implementing it across all sites. This can provide feedback as to whether the new practice is effective and also provide insight into the best way to implement the practice. Funds and programs need to recognize that this list will evolve as further work is done to identify what factors relate to positive participant outcomes.

The Means to Improve Participation

Should it prove to be the case that unmet demand exists, our review uncovered from related fields sets of activities that could be undertaken if increasing participation was a goal. Work in other areas demonstrates that perceptual factors are at least as important as physical barriers in forming an intention to participate, and both sets of factors can be manipulated to increase or target participation. Providers and decision makers seeking practical ways to increase enrollment and attendance in programs might consider these lessons learned from the job-training, military-recruiting, and OST fields. Proven or promising ways to bolster enrollment rates include identifying all possible participants, dedicating sufficient resources for outreach and recruitment, locating such efforts in places where targeted youth and their key influencers congregate, and combining advertising resources with other OST organizations. Monitoring attendance and quality, following up on absentees, and offering incentives to programs for achieving high attendance rates are potential ways to improve attendance.

Assuming that it is in the youth's interest to engage in OST programs, it might become very important to shift the focus from unbridled growth to promoting participation of targeted youth, and at levels sufficiently high to benefit them. This will in turn require a greater focus on understanding environmental barriers and intention issues. Future work in OST needs to focus on elucidating these processes and identifying ways to effectively intervene to strengthen intention of individuals to engage in OST activities.

Such work should involve collecting survey data to understand perceived benefits of particular OST programs, the key influencers with respect to OST policymaking and how supportive these key influencers are, and the perceived benefits from alternative uses of OST. This type of information—about beliefs, values, and attitudes—needs to be collected for targeted youth (since the particulars with respect to a given program can vary greatly across groups and regions) to fashion a message that can be used in designing an intervention to develop appropriate programs and "sell" them to targeted audiences.

Any efforts to significantly increase the number of slots available will have to confront the possibility of a quantity or quality trade-off. A significant push to increase the number of after-school and other OST program slots might detract from the equally important and necessary business of understanding and improving quality programming so as to elicit increased demand.

Capacity Building

We next turned to evidence that described methods decision makers and planners could use to help build the capacity to serve participants better. While some argue for increasing program-funding streams as the solution to assumed low capacity, the review provided some more thoughtful notions about how to improve and build capacity both of individual programs and across local, regional, and national markets.

Arguments were uncovered that point to the effectiveness of more-integrated approaches within locales, with collaboration, joint planning, and networking as important ways to further the debate as well as identifying shared challenges, best practices, and common interest among the groups involved. Historic examples reviewed showed the importance of evaluation, self-assessment, standards, and quality assurance to the development of other relevant fields. More-generic discussions pointed to the need for better incentives for improved performance and perhaps market-based relationships to engage competition as a way to increase performance.

These types of approaches, as with other approaches discussed previously, would take resources, time, effort, and commitment. Collaboration and joint planning must be supported with funds for the time of the people involved. Evaluation and self-assessment systems must be developed and used. In short, capacity must be created and supported with significant resources. The predominant underlying system of poor incentives for performance and lack of accountability probably cannot form the base for an effective improvement effort. Any moves toward capacity must address the underlying incentive system for performance.

Finally, given the level of the field, it seems prudent to think about local demonstrations of the types of system-building activities being advocated. If conducted with care and with an eye toward gaining lessons from serious evaluations, demonstrations could point the way to building better community infrastructure.

Summary of the Needed Elements of a Policy Debate

We summarize here some basic information requirements that need to be addressed if programming is to be improved and the current debate is to become more productive:

- local assessments, using surveys and other field instruments, to clarify demand for specific services by specific classes of clients and the level and quality of existing providers
- development of forums for public consideration of the results of such analyses
- creation of more systematic program evaluations with proper controls for self-selection and, where possible, the effect of participation levels; documentation of the impact of varying program elements or contexts; determination of the effects by age-group or class of participant; and attention to measuring cost effectiveness
- as there is little value to a strong evaluation of a weak intervention, these quality evaluations should be applied selectively to large, publicly funded programs; and, any well-designed and funded programs with potentially wide impact (see Walker, 2004, for ideas on selection)
- dissemination of standardized measures of participation levels and intensity that are regularly reported and aggregated, combined, when possible, with serious attention to participation effects in program evaluations
- development and dissemination of tools to collect and report cost information and compiling of information necessary to undertake cost-effectiveness evaluations with the ultimate goal of comparing OST programs to other alternatives
- development, demonstration, testing, and evaluation of practical and cost-effective means to improve participant recruitment and enrollment practices for targeted services
- development of effective forums and incentives to disseminate existing standards, guidelines, and best practices as they evolve or are uncovered through research
- support for collection and analysis of data for use in decision making about provision of services, stronger monitoring, assessment, and accountability based on those guidelines and practices, including stronger incentives for performance.

Appendix A

This appendix summarizes each of the literature reviews of OST program evaluations that precede this manuscript.

Fashola (1998)

Although the final version was not published until 2002, Fashola undertook the first systematic assessment of OST program impacts in the late 1990s. Specifically, Fashola reviewed evaluations of after-school and extended-school-day programs that had an educational focus and were used with at-risk students. The review was intended to identify programs with strong evidence of effectiveness and of replicability. In addition, the program evaluations had to provide enough information to measure effect sizes.

She found 34 program evaluations that met these criteria; many of them were used during the school day, or the after-school part of the program was not evaluated. These fell into five categories: language-arts after-school programs, study-skills programs, academic programs in other curriculum areas, tutoring programs for reading, and community-based programs.

While she notes that most of the evaluations did not meet minimal acceptable research standards, she tentatively concludes that there is some evidence that after-school programs might positively impact academic outcomes. Of the 11 programs that were evaluated in after-school settings, 6 showed some evidence of positive effect on an array of academic outcomes (depending on what the evaluation measured).

Scott-Little, Hamann, and Jurs (2002)

Scott-Little, Hamann, and Jurs undertook a fairly similar assessment of the literature, but with greater selectivity in terms of the rigor of the evaluation design. The authors performed a meta-evaluation, making judgments about the quality, merit, and worth of the evaluation, but were unable to perform a full meta-analysis due to lack of sufficient description and data in the evaluations reports. Twenty-three studies were identified that fit their selection criteria for evaluations of direct-service programs, excluding direct mentoring or tutoring. Of the 23 programs, only 15 reported outcome data for participants; the majority of these were either preexperimental (i.e., no control group was used) or quasi-experimental. Only two evaluations used an experimental design.

Like Fashola, they conclude that the overall story emerging from the literature is encouraging. In particular, they argue that results suggest that participants might score higher across a range of academic impacts and on measures of socioemotional functioning. Nonetheless, they note that further research is needed to draw firm conclusions about the impacts of after-school programs.

Hollister (2003)

The last major review released prior to the release of the 21st CCLC evaluation was by Hollister. To deal with selection bias in most data sources, Hollister restricted his assessment to only the most rigorous evaluation designs—experimental designs—of which he identified ten. Despite this restriction, he found that a number of the gold-standard evaluations suffered methodological flaws. For example, one study randomly assigned students applying to a program to the intervention or control group, thus ensuring that the two groups were similar in every way (including motivation to sign up). In the analysis, however, the treatment group included students who attended the program at least 50 percent of the time for some of the analysis and at least 80 percent of the time for other parts of the analysis. Students who signed up but did not attend and students who did attend but at low rates were included in the control group, thus undermining the strength of random-assignment design.

Overall, overlooking these types of study-design flaws, Hollister concluded that these programs did show a positive effect on some academic outcomes (including achievement tests, grades, and graduation) and some nonacademic outcomes (including substance use, hitting someone, skipping school, relationships with peers and parents, dropout and child-bearing, and police record). He also noted that there might be links between certain program components and outcomes. In particular, (1) mentoring or tutoring might have positive effects on academic and some nonacademic outcomes, (2) parent involvement and training are sometimes effective components for nonacademic outcomes, and (3) life-skills curricula might be effective for some out-of-school outcomes.

Lauer et al. (2003)

In "The Effectiveness of Out-of-School-Time Strategies in Assisting Low-Achieving Students in Reading and Mathematics: A Research Synthesis," the researchers asked, What was the effectiveness of OST strategies in assisting low-achieving or at-risk students in reading and mathematics? They turned to 56 studies (47 with reading outcomes and 33 with math outcomes) to address this question. They conclude that the programs in the aggregate were effective for low-performing and at-risk students. For reading outcomes, the results suggested that a reading intervention has an overall effect size of 0.06 to 0.13 for low-income or at-risk students; for mathematics intervention, the estimated effect size is 0.09 to 0.17. However, as we comment more on below, the quality of the 56 evaluations they assessed was very questionable, and the reader should view these conclusions as suggestive, at best.

A strength of this report is that it tested the potential role of different moderators or factors that influence the strength of the intervention or program effects. Reading interventions appeared to be most effective among early elementary-school students (K–2), where mathematics interventions had stronger effects among high-school students (9–12). For mathematics (but not reading), mixing academic and social activities appeared to be most effective. For reading, impacts were greatest for one-on-one tutoring interventions. Finally, programs that had more hours of instruction (more than 44 hours, but not more than 210 hours) had positive outcomes. (If real, such a pattern might reflect developmental differences in the value of social interaction with peers and appropriate duration or dosage; adolescents might require more variety of activities than early elementary-school students.)

We warn the reader against reading too much into these findings. Although the authors say they are undertaking a meta-analysis, meta-analysis is typically restricted only to studies that incorporate random assignment. Since the purpose of meta-analysis is to compute an average effect size across studies, the analyst needs to ensure that the studies are restricted to those that are able to ensure that selection bias is not influencing the estimated "effect." Yet only 9 of the 44 studies included in this meta-analysis claim to use random assignment, and the authors did not separately report effect sizes based on analysis of these 9 studies.

Miller (2003)

Critical Hours: Afterschool Programs and Educational Success, by Beth Miller, examined what the literature says about the link between OST and success, especially for early adolescents. The review included a summary of evaluations of after-school programs for school-age children and early adolescents (middle-school students). Miller drew stronger conclusions than earlier reviewers from the same research base about the positive impacts of these programs. Although she discusses some study limitations, the potential problems these limitations cast on being able to interpret program impacts was not sufficiently discussed.

References

AERA—*see* American Educational Research Association.

Afterschool Alliance, "Across Demographic and Party Lines, Americans Clamor for Safe, Enriching Afterschool Programs," *Afterschool Alert: Poll Report,* No. 6, 2003, http://www.afterschoolalliance.org/poll_jan_2004. pdf (as of June 2004).

———, homepage, 2004, http://www.afterschool.org/ (as of June 2004).

Alexander, N. P., "School-Age Child Care: Concerns and Challenges," *Young Children,* Vol. 42, No. 1, 1986, pp. 3–12.

American Educational Research Association, "Class Size: Counting Students Can Count," *Research Points,* Vol. 1, No. 2, 2003, pp. 1–4. Online at http://www.aera.net/pubs/rp/RPFall03ClassSize-PDF2.pdf (as of June 2004).

Angrist, J. D., and V. Lavy, "Does Teacher Training Affect Pupil Learning? Evidence from Matched Comparisons in Jerusalem Public Schools," NBER Working Paper No. 6781, 1998.

Attorney General of the State of California, Proposition 49, *Before and After School Programs, State Grants, Initiative Statute, Official Title and Summary.* Sacramento, Calif.: Department of State, 2002. Online at http://www. ss.ca.gov/elections/bp_ge02/prop49.pdf (as of June 2004).

Backer, T. E., *Strengthening Nonprofits Capacity Building and Philanthropy,* Encino, Calif.: Human Interaction Research Institute, 2000.

———, "Practical Strategies for Change: Collaboration, Systems Change and Sustainability," speech given at the Frequent Users of Health Services Initiative Luncheon, June 27, 2003, Encino, Calif.: Human Interaction Research Institute.

Beckett, M., "Don't Make After-School Care the Next Big Myth," *RAND Review*, December 2002, p.30.

————. "Monitor After-School Care Programs Carefully," *San Diego Tribune*, January 2, 2003, p. B-9.

Beckett, M., A. Hawken, and A. Jacknowitz, *Accountability for After-School Care: Devising Standards and Measuring Adherence to Them*, Santa Monica, Calif.: RAND Corporation, MR-1411-SSCCP, 2001.

Belle, D., "Varieties of Self-Care: A Qualitative Look at Children's Experiences in the After-School Hours," *Merrill Palmer Quarterly*, Vol. 43, No. 3, 1997, pp. 478–496.

Blau, David, and Janet Currie, "Preschool, Day Care, and After School Care: Who's Minding the Kids?" June 2003, http://www.econ.ucla.edu/people/papers/Currie/currie291.pdf (as of June 2004).

Blum, R. W., and P. M. Rinehart, *Reducing the Risk: Connections That Make a Difference in the Lives Of Youth*, Minneapolis: Division of General Pediatrics and Adolescent Health, University of Minnesota, 1997.

Bohrnstedt, G., and B. Stecher, *What We Have Learned about Class Size Reduction in California*, Palo Alto, Calif.: California Department of Education, 2002.

Booth, A., and J. Dunn, *Family-School Links: How Do They Affect Educational Outcomes?*, Hillsdale, N.J.: Lawrence Erlbaum Associates, 1996.

Brewer, D. J., C. Krop, B. P. Gill, and R. Reichardt, "How Much Does It Cost to Reduce Class Size? A National Perspective," *Educational Evaluation and Policy Analysis*, Vol. 21, No. 2, 1999, pp. 179–192.

Buchmann, Claudia, "Getting Ahead in Kenya: Social Capital, Shadow Education, and Achievement," in Bruce Fuller and Emily Hannum, eds., *Research in Sociology of Education*, Vol. 14: *Schooling and Social Capital in Diverse Cultures*, London: Elsevier Science, 2002.

Casper, L. M., and M. O'Connell, "State Estimates of Organized Child Care Facilities," Washington, D.C.: U.S. Bureau of the Census, 1998.

Chaplin, D., and M. J. Puma, "What 'Extras' Do We Get with Extracurriculars? Technical Research Considerations," Washington, D.C.: Urban Institute, 2003.

Chaput, S. S., Harvard Family Research Project, "Characterizing and Measuring Participation in Out-of-School Time Programs," *The Evaluation Exchange,* Vol. X, No. 1, Spring 2004, pp. 2–3.

Chaput, Sandra Simpkins, Priscilla Little, and Heather Weiss, "Understanding and Measuring Attendance in Out of School Time Programs," *Issues and Opportunities in Out of School Time Evaluation,* No. 7, August 2004.

Children Now, *After School Care in California: An Overview,* Oakland, Calif.: Children Now, 2001.

Clark, R. M., *Family Life and School Achievement: Why Poor Black Children Succeed or Fail,* Chicago: University of Chicago Press, 1983.

Clayton, R. R., A. Cattarello, L. E. Day, and K. P. Walden, "Persuasive Communications and Drug Abuse Prevention: An Evaluation of the DARE program," in L. Donohew, H. Sypher, and W. Bukowski, eds., *Persuasive Communication and Drug Abuse Prevention,* Hillsdale, N.J.: Lawrence Erlbaum Associates, 1991, pp. 295–313.

Comer, J. P., "Educating Poor Minority Children," *Scientific American,* Vol. 259, No. 5, 1988, pp. 42–48.

Connell, J., M. Gambone, and T. Smith, *Youth Development in Community Settings: Challenges to Our Field and Our Approach,* Community Action for Youth Project, Toms River, N.J.: 2000.

Costello, C. B., V. R. Wight, and A. J. Stone, eds., *The American Woman 2003–2004: Daughters of a Revolution—Young Women Today,* Women's Research and Education Institute, Washington, D.C.: Palgrave Macmillan, 2003.

Dertouzos, J. N., and S. Garber, *Is Military Advertising Effective? An Estimation Methodology and Applications to Recruiting in the 1980s and 90s,* Santa Monica, Calif.: RAND Corporation, MR-1591, 2003.

Dishion, T. J., J. McCord, and F. Poulin, "When Interventions Harm," *American Psychologist,* Vol. 54, No. 9, 1999, pp. 755–764.

Dishion, T. J., G. R. Patteron, M. Stoolmiller, and M. L. Skinner, "Family, School, and Behavioral Antecedents to Early Adolescent Involvement with Antisocial Peers," *Developmental Psychology,* Vol. 27, 1991, pp. 172–180.

DOEd—*see* U.S. Department of Education.

Duffett, Ann, and Jean Johnson, *All Work and No Play? Listening to What Kids and Parents Really Want from Out-of-School Time,* New York: Public Agenda, 2004.

Dynarski, Mark, "It Feels Fine Once You Get Used to It: Lessons from the 21st Century National Evaluation," remarks presented at the Brooking Institution's Stakeholder Forum on After School Programs, Washington, D.C., July 10, 2003.

Dynarski, Mark, Susanne Jame-Burdumy, Mary Moore, Linda Rosenberg, John Drake, and Wendy Mansfield, *When Schools Stay Open Late: The Evaluation of the 21st Century Community Learning Centers Programs: New Findings,* Washington, D.C.: U.S. Government Printing Office, 2004.

Eccles J., "Percieved Control and the Development of Academic Motivation," *Monographs of the Society for Research in Child Development,* Vol. 63, No. 2–3, 1998, pp. 221–231.

Eccles, J. S., S. Lord, and C. Midgley, "What Are We Doing to Early Adolescents? The Impact of Educational Contexts on Early Adolescents," *American Journal of Education,* Vol. 99, 1991, pp. 521–542.

Epstein, J. L., and S. L. Dauber, "School Programs and Teacher Practices of Parent Involvement in Inner-City Elementary and Middle Schools," *Elementary School Journal,* 1991, pp. 289–305.

Farkas, Steve, Ann Duffett, and Jean Johnson, *Necessary Compromises: How Parents, Employers and Child's Advocates View Child Care Today,* New York: Public Agenda, 2000.

Fashola, O. S., *Review of Extended-Day and After-School Programs and Their Effectiveness,* Baltimore, Md.: Center for Research on the Education of Students Placed at Risk, 1998.

Fiester, Leila, *A Guide to Issues and Strategies for Monitoring Attendance in Afterschool and other Youth Programs,* Afterschool Counts, Washington, D.C.: Policy Studies Associates, 2004.

Fine, M., *Framing Dropouts: Notes on the Politics of an Urban High School,* Albany: State University of New York Press, 1991.

Fishbein, M., "The Role of Theory in HIV prevention," *AIDS Care,* Vol. 12, No. 3, 2000, pp. 273–278.

Fishbein, M., H. C. Triandis, F. H. Kanfer, M. Becker, S. E. Middlestadt, and A. Eichler, "Factors Influencing Behavior and Behavior Change," in A. Baum, T. A. Revenson, and J. E. Singer, eds., *Handbook of Health Psychology,* Mahwah, N.J.: Lawrence Erlbaum Associates, 2001, pp. 3–16.

Forum for Youth Investment————, "Quality Counts, but Does It Sell?" *Forum Focus*, Vol. 1, Issue 1, 2003, pp. 1–2.

Fricker, R. D., and C. C. Fair, *Going to the Mines to Look for Diamonds: Experimenting with Military Recruiting Stations in Malls,* Santa Monica, Calif.: RAND Corporation, MR-1697-OSD, 2003.

Furstenberg, F. F., Jr., T. D. Cook, J. Eccles, G. H. Elder Jr., and A. Sameroff, *Managing to Make It: Urban Families and Adolescent Success,* Chicago: University of Chicago Press, 1999.

Gambone, Michelle, Adena Klem, and James Connell, *Finding Out What Matters for Youth: Testing Links in a Community Action Framework for Youth Development,* Philadelphia: Youth Development Strategies and Institute for Research and Reform in Education, 2002.

GAO—*see* U.S. General Accounting Office.

Glass, G. V., L. S. Cahen, M. L. Smith, and N. N. Filby, *School Class Size: Research and Policy,* Beverly Hills, Calif.: Sage, 1982.

Glass, G. V., and M. L. Smith, "Meta-analysis of Research on Class Size and Achievement," *Educational Evaluation and Policy Analysis,* Vol. 1, No. 1, 1979, pp. 2–16.

Goodman, W., "Boom In Day Care Industry the Result of Many Social Changes," *Monthly Labor Review,* August 1995, pp. 3–12.

Governor's Crime Commission, *After School Program Handbook: Strategies and Effective Practice,* North Carolina Department of Crime Control and Public Safety, 1998.

Granger, R. C., and T. Kane, "Improving the Quality of After-School Programs," *Education Week,* Vol. 23, Issue 23, 2004, pp. 52, 76.

Grissmer, D., A. Flanagan, J. Kawata, and S. Williamson, *Improving Student Achievement: What State NAEP Test Scores Tell Us,* Santa Monica, Calif.: RAND Corporation, MR-924-EDU, 2000.

Grossman, A., "Philanthropic Social Capital Markets: Performance Driven Philanthropy," Harvard Business School, Social Enterprise Series, No. 12, unpublished working paper, 1999.

Grossman, J. B., and J. E. Rhodes, *The Test of Time: Predictors and the Effects of Duration in Youth Mentoring Relationships,* Philadelphia: Public/Private Ventures, 1999.

Grossman, J. B., et al. *Multiple Choices after School: Findings from the Extended-Service Schools Initiative,* Philadelphia: Public/Private Ventures, 2002.

Grotevant, H. D., "Adolescent Development in Family Context," in N. Eisenberg, ed., *Handbook of Child Psychology: Social, Emotional, and Personality Development,* New York: John Wiley and Sons, 1998, pp. 1,097–1,149.

Halpern, R., "After-School Programs for Low-Income Children: Promise and Challenge," *Future of Families,* Vol. 9, No. 20, 1999, pp. 81–95.

———, "The Promise of After-School Programs for Low-Income Children," *Early Childhood Research Quarterly,* Vol. 15, No. 2, 2000, pp. 185–214.

———, "A Different Kind of Child Development Institution: The History of After-School Programs for Low-Income Children," *Teachers College Record,* Vol. 104, No. 2, 2002, pp. 178–211.

Halpern, R., J. Spielberger, and S. Rob, *Evaluation of the MOST (Making the Most of Out-of-School Time) Initiative: Final Report and Summary of Findings,* Chapin Hall Center for Children, 2001, pp. 14–25.

Hamilton, G., and S. Scrivener, *Promoting Participation: How to Increase Involvement in Welfare-to-Work Activities,* New York: Manpower Demonstration Research Corporation, 1999.

Haycock, K., "Closing the Achievement Gap," *Educational Leadership,* Vol. 58, No. 6, 2001, pp. 6–11.

Heaviside, S., E. Farris, C. Dunn, R. Fry, and J. Carpenter, *Services and Resources for Children and Young Adults in Public Libraries: Fast Response Survey System,* Washington, D.C.: U.S. Department of Education, Office of Educational Research and Improvement, Educational Resources Information Center, National Center for Education Statistics, NCES 95–357, 1995.

Henderson, A. T., and N. Berla, *A New Generation of Evidence: The Family Is Critical to Academic Achievement,* Washington, D.C.: Center for Law and Education, 1994.

Hobbs, B. H., "Increasing the 4-H Participation of Youth from High-Risk Environments," *Journal of Extension,* Vol. 37, No. 4, 1999. Online at http://joe.org/joe/1999august/rb1.html (as of June 2004).

Hofferth, S. L., A. Brayfield, S. Deich, and P. Holcomb, *National Child Care Survey, 1990,* Washington, D.C.: Urban Institute, 1991.

Hofferth, S. L., and J. F. Sandberg, "How American Children Spend Their Time," *Journal of Marriage and Family*, Vol. 63, No. 2, 2001, pp. 295–308.

Hollister, R., *The Growth in After-School Programs and Their Impact*, Washington, D.C.: Brookings Roundtable on Children, 2003.

House, J. D. "The Relationship Between Academic Self-Concept, Achievement-Related Expectancies, and College Attrition," *Journal of College Student Development*, Vol. 33, 1992a, pp. 5–10.

———, "The Relationship Between Task Competence, Achievement Expectancies, and School Withdrawal of Academically Unprepared Adolescent Students," *Child Study Journal*, Vol. 22, 1992b, pp. 253–272.

Hustman, W. Z., "Constraints to Activity Participation in Early Adolescence," *Journal of Early Adolescence*, Vol. 12, 1992, pp. 280–299.

Jackson, A. W., and G. A. Davis, *Turning Points 2000: Educating Adolescents in the 21st Century*, report of the Carnegie Corporation, New York: Teachers College Press, 2000.

Jacob, B. A., and L. Lefgren, "The Impact of Teacher Training on Student Achievement: Quasi-experimental Evidence from School Reform Efforts in Chicago," NBER Working Paper no. w8916, 2002.

Joblessness and Urban Poverty Research Program, "After-School Time," Urban Seminar Series on Children's Health and Safety, May 10–11, 2001, http://www.ksg.harvard.edu/urbanpoverty/Sitepages/UrbanSeminar/OutofSchool/aftsch.htm (as of June 2004).

Johnson, K., D. Bryant, T. Strader, G. Bucholtz, M. Berbaum, D. Collins, and T. Noe, "Reducing Alcohol and Other Drug Use by Strengthening Community, Family, and Youth Resiliency: An Evaluation of the Creating Lasting Connections Program," *Journal of Adolescent Research*, Vol. 11, No. 1, 1996, pp. 36–67.

Kane, T., "The Impact of After-School Programs: Interpreting the Results of Four Recent Evaluations," New York: William T. Grant Foundation, 2004.

Krueger, A., "Experimental Estimates of Education Production Functions," *Quarterly Journal of Economics*, Vol. 114, No. 2, 1999, pp. 497–532.

Lauer, P. A., Motoko Akiba, Stephanie Wilkerson, Helen Apthorp, David Snow, and Mya Martin-Glenn, *The Effectiveness of Out-of-School-Time*

Strategies in Assisting Low-Achieving Students in Reading and Mathematics: A Research Synthesis, Aurora, Colo.: MCREL, 2003.

Lauver, Sherri, Pricilla Little, and Heather Weiss, "Moving Beyond the Barriers: Attracting and Sustaining Youth Participation in Out-of-School Time Programs," *Issues and Opportunities in Out-Of-School Time Evaluation*, No. 6, 2004.

Linnell, D., *Evaluation of Capacity Building: Lessons from the Field*, Washington, D.C.: Alliance for Nonprofit Management, 2004.

Littell, J., and J. Wynn, "The Availability and Use of Community Resources for Young Adolescents in an Inner-City and a Suburban Community," Chicago: Chapin Hall Center for Children at University of Chicago, 1989.

Little, Priscilla, and Erin Harris, "A Review of Out-of-School Time Program Quasi-experimental and Experimental Evaluation Results," *Out-of-School Time Snapshot*, No. 1, 2003.

Lugaila, Terry, *A Child's Day: 2000 (Selected Indicators of Child Well-Being)*, Current Population Reports, Washington D.C.: U.S. Bureau of the Census, 2003.

Maxfield, M., A. Schirm, and N. Rodriguez-Planas, *The Quantum Opportunity Program Demonstration: Implementation and Short-Term Impacts*, Washington, D.C.: Mathematica Policy Research, 2003.

Miller, B. M., *Critical Hours: Afterschool Programs and Educational Success*, Quincy, Mass.: Nellie Mae Education Foundation, 2003.

Miller, B. M., and F. Marx, "After-School Arrangements in Middle Childhood: A Review of the Literature (Action Research Paper No. 2)," Wellesley, Mass.: Wellesley College Center for Research on Women, School-Age Child Care Project, 1990.

Molnar, A., "Evaluating the SAGE Program: A Pilot Program in Targeted Pupil-Teacher Reduction in Wisconsin," *Educational Evaluation and Policy Analysis*, Vol. 21, No. 2, 1999, pp. 165–178.

Myers, D., and A. Schirm, *The Impacts of Upward Bound: Final Report for Phase I of the National Evaluation*, Washington, D.C.: U.S. Department of Education, Planning and Evaluation Service, 1999.

NAESP—*see* National Association of Elementary School Principals.

National Association of Elementary School Principals, *After-School Programs and the K–8 Principal: Standards for Quality School-Age Child Care,* rev. ed., Alexandria, Va.: National Association of Elementary School Principals, 1999.

National Institute on Out-of-School Time, *Making an Impact on Out of-School Time,* Wellesley, Mass.: Wellesley College Center for Research on Women, National Institute on Out-of-School Time, 2000.

National Research Council, Committee on Developing a Research Agenda on the Education of Limited-English-Proficient and Bilingual Students, *Improving Schooling for Language-Minority Children: A Research Agenda,* Diane August and Kenji Hakuta, eds., Washington, D.C.: National Academies Press, 1997.

National Research Council and Institute of Medicine, *After-School Programs to Promote Child and Adolescent Development: Summary of a Workshop,* Jennifer A. Gootman, ed., Washington, D.C.: National Academies Press, 2000.

———, *Community Programs to Promote Youth Development,* J. Eccles and J. A. Gootman, eds., Washington, D.C.: National Academies Press, 2002.

National School-Age Care Alliance, *The National School-Age Care Alliance Standards for Quality School-Age Care,* Boston: National School-Age Care Alliance, 1998.

Newman, R. P., S. M. Smith, and R. A. Murphy, *Matter of Money: The Cost and Financing of Youth Development,* Washington, D.C.: Center for Youth Development and Policy Research, Academy for Educational Development, 1999.

NIOST—*see* National Institute on Out-of-School Time.

NRC—*see* National Research Council.

NSACA—*see* National School-Age Care Alliance.

O'Neill, G., and M. O'Connell, "State Estimates of Child Care Establishments: 1977–1997," Washington, D.C.: U.S. Bureau of the Census, 2001.

Padgette, H. C., *A Guide to Federal Sources for Out-of-School-Time and Community School Initiatives,* New York: Finance Project, 2003.

Philliber, S., K. J. Williams, S. Herrling, and E. West, "Preventing Pregnancy and Improving Health Care Access among Teenagers: An Evaluation of the Children's Aid Society—Carrera Program," *Perspectives on Sexual and Reproductive Health,* Vol. 34, No. 5, 2002, pp. 244–251.

Pierce, Kim M., Jill V. Hamm, and Deborah L. Vandell, "Experiences in After-School Programs and Children's Adjustment in First-Grade Classrooms," *Child Development,* Vol. 80, No. 3, 1999, pp. 756–767.

Pittman, K., M. Irby, and T. Ferber, *Unfinished Business: Further Reflections on a Decade of Promoting Youth Development,* Washington, D.C.: International Youth Foundation, 2000.

Pittman, Karen, Alicia Wilson-Ahlstrom, and Nicole Yohalem, "Reflections on System Building: Lessons from the After-School Movement," *Out-of School Time Policy Commentary,* Forum for Youth Development, No. 3, 2003.

Purkey, S. C., and M. S. Smith, "Effective Schools: A Review," *Elementary School Journal,* Vol. 83, No. 4, 1983, pp. 427–452.

Quinn, J., "Where Need Meets Opportunity: Youth Development Programs for Early Teens," in R. Behrman, ed., *The Future of Children: When School Is Out,* Washington, D.C.: David and Lucile Packard Foundation, 1999, pp. 104–113.

Reisner, E. R., C. A. Russell, M. E. Welsh, J. Birmingham, and R. N. White, *Supporting Quality and Scale in After-School Services to Urban Youth: Evaluation of Program Implementation and Student Engagement in TASC After-School Program's Third Year,* Washington, D.C.: Policy Studies Associates, 2002.

Roberts, G. C., and D. C. Treasure, "Children in Sport," *Sport Science Review,* Vol. 2, 1992, pp. 46–64.

Roderick, M., *The Path to Dropping Out: Evidence for Intervention,* Cambridge, Mass.: Harvard University, John F. Kennedy School of Government, 1991.

Rosenthal, R., and D. L. Vandell, "Quality of Care at School-Aged Child-Care Programs: Regulatable Features, Observed Experiences, Child Perspectives and Parent Perspectives," *Child Development,* Vol. 67, 1996, pp. 2,434–2,445.

Roth, J., and J. Brooks-Gunn, "Youth Development Programs: Risk, Prevention and Policy," *Journal of Adolescent Health,* Vol. 32, 2003, pp. 170–182.

Roth, J., J. Brooks-Gunn, L. Murray, and W. Foster, "Promoting Healthy Adolescents: Synthesis of Youth Development Program Evaluations," *Journal of Research on Adolescence,* Vol. 8, 1998, pp. 423–459.

Sackett, P. R., and A. Mavor, eds., *Attitudes, Aptitudes, and Aspirations of American Youth: Implications for Military Recruitment,* Washington, D.C.: National Academies Press, 2003.

Schinke, S. P., G. J. Botvin, J. E. Trimble, M. A. Orlandi, L. D. Gilchrist, and V. S. Locklear, "Preventing Substance Abuse among American Indian Adolescents: A Bicultural Competence Skill Approach," *Journal of Counseling Psychology,* Vol. 35, No. 1, 1988, pp. 87–90.

Schumacher, R., K. Irish, and J. Lombardi, "Meeting Great Expectations: Integrating Early Education Program Standards in Child Care," Washington, D.C.: Foundation for Child Development, 2003.

Scott-Little, C., M. S. Hamann, and S. G. Jurs, "Evaluations of After-School Programs: A Meta-evaluation of Methodologies and Narrative Synthesis of Findings," *American Journal of Evaluation,* Vol. 23, No. 4, 2002, pp. 387–419.

Searle, M. S., and E. L. Jackson, "Socioeconomic Variations in Perceived Barriers to Recreation Participation among Would-Be Participants," *Leisure Sciences,* Vol. 7, No. 2, 1985, pp. 227–259.

Seefeldt, V., M. Ewing, and S. Walk, *Overview of Youth Sports Programs in the United States,* Washington, D.C.: Carnegie Council on Adolescent Development, 1993.

Seppanen, P. S., J. Love, D. deVries, L. Bernstein, M. Seligson, F. Marx, and E. Kisker, *National Study of Before- and After-School Programs,* Washington, D.C.: U.S. Department of Education, 1993.

Skillman Foundation, *Recreating Recreation in Detroit, Hamtramack and Highland Park,* Detroit, Mich.: Skillman Foundation, 1995.

Smith, C., M. L. Denton, R. Faris, and M. Regnerus, "Mapping American Adolescent Religious Participation," *Journal for the Scientific Study of Religion,* Vol. 41, No. 4, 2002, pp. 597–612. Online at http://www.youth andreligion.org/publications/docs/JSSR_article.pdf.

Smoll, F. L., R. E. Smith, N. P., Barnett, and J. J. Everett, "Enhancement of Children's Self-Esteem through Social Support and Training for Youth Sport Coaches," *Journal of Applied Psychology,* Vol. 78, 1993, pp. 602–610.

Snydner, T., *120 Years of American Education,* Washington, D.C.: National Center for Education Statistics, 1993.

Steinberg, L., "We Know Some Things: Parent-Adolescent Relations in Retrospect and Prospect," *Journal of Research in Adolescence,* Vol. 11, No. 1, 2001, pp. 1–19.

Stoney, L., *Looking into New Mirrors: Lessons of Early Childhood Finance and System-Building,* Washington, D.C.: National Child Care Information Center at the Department of Health and Human Services, 1998. Online at http://nccic.org/pubs/mirrors/preface.html.

Tolman, J., K. Pittman, N. Yohalem, J. Thomases, and M. Trammel, *Moving an Out-of-School Agenda: Lessons and Challenges Across Cities,* Takoma Park, Md.: Forum for Youth Investment, 2002.

U.S. Census Bureau, *Statistical Abstract of the U.S: 2003.* Washington, D.C.: U.S. Government Printing Office, 2003.

U.S. Department of Education, Office of the Under Secretary, "When Schools Stay Open Late: The National Evaluation of the 21st Century Community Learning Centers Program: First Year Findings," Washington, D.C.: U.S. Government Printing Office, 2003.

————, National Center for Education Statistics, "Before- and After-School Care, Programs, and Activities of Children in Kindergarten Through Eighth Grade: 2001," in B. Kleiner, M. J. Nolin, and C. Chapman, *NCES 2004–008,* Washington, D.C.: 2004.

U.S. Department of Education and U.S. Department of Justice, *Working for Children and Families: Safe and Smart After-School Programs,* Washington, D.C.: U.S. Government Printing Office, 2000. Online at http://www.ed.gov/offices/OESE/archives/pubs/parents/SafeSmart/green-1.doc (as of June 2004).

U.S. General Accounting Office, *Youth Illicit Drug Use Prevention: DARE Long-Term Evaluations and Federal Efforts,* Washington, D.C.: U.S. Government Printing Office, 2003.

Vandell, D. L., and L. Shumow, "After-School Child Care Programs," *Future of Children,* Vol. 9, No. 2, 1999, pp. 64–80.

Vandell, Deborah, et al., *The Study of Promising After-School Programs Descriptive Report of the Promising Programs,* Washington, D.C.: Policy Studies Associates, 2004.

VanderWood, Jerry, "Aggregate Lessons Learned on the Use of Data, Communications and Political Strategizing by Local Urban Health Initiative Campaigns," paper presented at Urban Seminar Series on Children's Health and Safety, Harvard University, December 4–5, 2003.

Walker, Gary, "Ensuring the Success of After-School Programs," *Notebook, Grant Makers for Education,* summer 2004, p. 4.

Wechsler, S., *Meeting the Challenge: Financing Out-of-School Time Programming in Boston and Massachusetts,* Boston, Mass.: Parents United for Child Care, 2001.

Weiss, F. L., and H. J. Nicholson, "Friendly PEERsuasion Against Substance Use: The Girls Incorporated Model and Evaluation," in J. Valentine, J. A. De Jong, and N. J. Kennedy, eds., *Substance Abuse Prevention in Multicultural Communities,* Binghamton, N.Y.: Haworth Press, 1998, pp. 7–22.

Weiss, Heather, and Priscilla Little, Harvard Family Research Project, "Why, When, and How to Use Evaluation: Experts Speak Out," *Issues and Opportunities in Out-of-School Time Evaluation,* No. 5, 2003.

Wilson-Ahlstrom, A., T. Ferber, K. Pittman, and M. Irby, "Fast Forward: A Background Paper Prepared for the Packard Foundation's After-School YouthVisioning Meeting," Washington, D.C.: Forum for Youth Investment, 2002.

Wynn, J. R., "The Role of Local Intermediary Organizations in the Youth Development Field," discussion paper prepared for the Edna McConnell Clark Foundation, University of Chicago, Chicago: Chapin Hall Center for Children, 2000.

Zigler, E., and S. Muenchow, *Head Start: The Inside Story of America's Most Successful Educational Experiment,* New York: Basic Books, 1992.

Zill, N., C. W. Nord, and L. S. Loomis, *Adolescent Time Use, Risky Behavior, and Outcomes: An Analysis of National Data,* Rockville, Md.: Westat, 1995.